Shamanism: The Book of Journeys

First published by O Books, 2010
O Books is an imprint of John Hunt Publishing Ltd., The Bothy, Deershot Lodge, Park Lane, Ropley, Hants, SO24 0BE, UK
office1@o-books.net
www.o-books.net

Distribution in:

UK and Europe
Orca Book Services
orders@orcabookservices.co.uk
Tel: 01202 665432 Fax: 01202 666219
Int. code (44)

USA and Canada
NBN
custserv@nbnbooks.com
Tel: 1 800 462 6420 Fax: 1 800 338 4550

Australia and New Zealand
Brumby Books
sales@brumbybooks.com.au
Tel: 61 3 9761 5535 Fax: 61 3 9761 7095

Far East (offices in Singapore, Thailand, Hong Kong, Taiwan)
Pansing Distribution Pte Ltd
kemal@pansing.com
Tel: 65 6319 9939 Fax: 65 6462 5761

South Africa
Stephan Phillips (pty) Ltd
Email: orders@stephanphillips.com
Tel: 27 21 4489839 Telefax: 27 21 4479879

Design: Stuart Davies

ISBN: 978 1 84694 357 7

A CIP catalogue record for this book is available from the British Library.

Printed by Digital Book Print

Shamanism: The Book of Journeys

Robert Levy & Dr. Eve Bruce

BOOKS

Winchester, UK
Washington, USA

CONTENTS

Dedication

To all who walk in gratitude with the knowledge that we are indigenous to this Earth, our mother – the Earth honoring people walking the Shamanic path. To those of you who find the courage to walk in the mystery that we call life, and death. It is to all of you that we dedicate this book, and it is our hope that our journeys will make your journey a little easier.

Acknowledgements

Robert Levy

I have been blessed with having come into contact with so many shamanic practitioners and teachers that it is difficult for me to know where to begin. Within this text, Eve and I state that Spirit embodies love, understanding and compassion. And I may add a fourth to that – patience. Those that I have met that I call both teachers and friends each are abundantly endowed with those four characteristics. It is because of them I have reached this point on my shamanic path.

To begin at the beginning, I thank Aimee Morgan and Hanakia Zedek. I thank John Perkins, without whom I would never have reached the dreams I set for myself. I thank Llyn Roberts, Tom Cowan, Christina Pratt, Nan Moss, David Corbin, John Matthews, Alberto Villoldo, Michael Harner, Robert Moss and Hank Wasselman for sharing with me the knowledge and wisdom they each possess. I thank the people who, along with me, organized the New York Shamanic Circle and I thank the people who came to our circles to find their own healing as well as to help heal those around them.

To Ipupiara Makunaiman and Claicha Toscano – whatever I do and accomplish as I walk this shamanic path, is due to your friendship, guidance and the faith you placed in an assistant!

To Victoria Botero, who chastised me for not acknowledging her in my first book. For that oversight, I take full responsibility and hereby acknowledge her in this book.

To Dr. Eve Bruce, my love, my gratitude, my thank you. Without you, without your teachings, this book could never have been written. With you, a dream that existed only in Spirit reality is now being birthed in our reality. Eve, we have a child!

And finally, to my wife, Shigeko. You have filled my life with joy and happiness, and without that I would not have been able to complete this book. Thank you for feeling obligated for going on our second date, and beginning with me the journey in life that we now share.

Eve Bruce

I give thanks to those above for all your teachings and wisdom. Special thanks for the endless patience of Robert, for waiting while life's tasks as a mother made writing this book take far longer than he had hoped, for never giving up, and for pushing me to write this with him.

To my soul family, my brothers and sisters without whom I would be lost.

To Ipupiara Makunaiman, Jenny Clay Toscano, John Perkins. To Vusamazulu Credo Mutwa, Taita Esteban Tamayo, Grandmother Lillian Pitawanakwat, Taita Alberto Taxo, Uishin Daniel Wachapa, Paje Shore, and Maestre Barata.

I could never name all who have taught me so much along the way, but know that I hold you all in my heart and soul, and that we are one.

To my blood family for all their support and love: Alice, Michael, Coale and Jock; and to my beautiful granddaughters Blake, Morgan, Olivia, Lauren, Zoe, and Cecelia.

To my soulmate, Michael, who makes this Earthly walk through life filled with love.

The materials presented in this book are the opinions of its authors. This book is intended to offer alternative ways of attacking various problems our readers may face. The material within is for informational purposes. It is not intended to replace conventional therapy but rather add to those therapies. The reader accepts the responsibility for applying the information presented and for using the techniques given within the book.

To Reiki and other energy practitioners – to traditional therapists who wish to explore introducing the shamanic journey into their practice:

The book, *Shamanic Reiki, Expanded Ways of Working with Universal Life Force Energy,* by Llyn Roberts and Robert Levy, details how incorporating shamanic techniques can easily and effectively be added to your practice. All the journeys in this book can be used within that context. For those readers who wish to do so, and who have not read *Shamanic Reiki,* Robert suggests that you consider it.

Preface

Robert

During the summer of 2007, I was assisting John Perkins (www.johnperkins.org) at Omega Institute, Rhinebeck, NY, in teaching a shamanic workshop. While speaking with a participant about his issue, and after I suggested a journey he could do to find possibilities for solving it, the participant asked me, 'Is there a book of journeys that I can buy that will help me?' My answer was no, but the seed that eventually grew into this book was planted.

Shamanism, as a spiritual practice, is experiencing a revival in our western culture. Many people are finding that the time honored ways our far ancestors and current indigenous people connect to Spirit can fit harmoniously into our lives to help promote both physical and emotional healing. All a person need do to find the accuracy of that statement is look in any book store to see how many books are currently available that dissect shamanism from every angle. But, there is one aspect that is missing.

The workhorse of shamanism is the shamanic journey. It is the way most shamanic practitioners access both spirit and the alternate reality where the helping spirits live and thrive. Though simple, because we westerners tend to feel with our heads instead of our hearts, most people complicate the process. Many books on shamanism include ideas for shamanic journeys and give examples. But to find them, a reader has to read the book and make their own notes of the journeys they read about. What is lacking in the published field is a book of journeys, a reference that practitioners of any level can use to give them ideas of various journeys that can help them draw a direct line from spirit to the issue they are working on. That lack was apparent in the eyes of the participant from John's workshop.

Dr. Eve Bruce has gracefully accepted the title of co-author. Eve, author of *Shaman MD*, has been my teacher, mentor and then friend for many years. It was partly because of her that I was able to find my shamanic legs while assisting her in her workshops at Omega Institute. For me, Eve embraces the same qualities that we give to spirit Herself: Love, Understanding, and Compassion. She has been a shamanic practitioner much longer than me; she has trained with indigenous shamans, and understands that sacred does not mean solemn, and never misses a chance to laugh. What better person is there to add her wonderful expertise to the idea of this – a book of journeys?

Eve

When Robert first approached me to write this book with him, I hesitated. I did not have the time; I had other projects that were calling to me; I didn't know if I could write with another person... All the excuses! We both journeyed, and Robert was told that I would write, but would not be as committed to it – at first. I was told to write it. Period. And so we began.

During the writing I found out how perfect we were as a team, not just because of the male/female perspective, although there is that. We were perfect because we approach shamanism – and journeying – very differently. I was brought up in East Africa, and have spent most of my time training outside of the United States, in the jungles of South America, in Africa, in the Himalayas. And when I study in North America, it is with native peoples.

Robert was integral in founding one of the oldest journey groups that I know of in an urban setting, New York City. He is careful, kind, patient and filled with integrity.

Bringing together the urban and native ways of journeying is what I found most interesting. In the urban setting journeys tend to have a defined purpose intellectually, and are extremely fruitful in psychological development. In native settings there is also an intent; however, I find that more is left to spirit, and sometimes journeys are simply to bring in energy and story – and to engender a sense of blissful connection – a kind of worship if you will. Urban journeying takes time, and is usually with a drum or rattle. Native journeying may also be done in this manner; however, it is more a way of life, a continual journey walking between the worlds. This text is certain to be for an audience from industrialized countries, and so it is perfect to have these two perspectives about journeying, and about shamanic practice.

It is my hope that, in whatever small way that I can, I will contribute to bringing back the wisdom of the indigenous peoples. That this book will inspire you to listen to those who walked before you, and to those still living in native ways, for current native peoples often do so at great personal and communal sacrifice. That this book will help you to find your own indigenous nature. That together we can honor our Mother Earth and Father Sky, thus coming together to build the New Earth.

This text is a reference. Just as a beginner cook who, going through cookbooks in order to learn new dishes and to find a recipe, will follow it exactly as written at first, and then over time flip through for ideas rather than to learn new dishes. Just as a more experienced cook will use a reference more for inspiration than exact instruction and, with more time and practice in cooking, recipes are used as templates and modified ad lib. Eventually, a chef will rarely use a cookbook at all. Similarly, this cookbook of journeys is meant to be useful for all levels of shamanic journeying; for learning, for inspiration and ideas, and to be modified as spirit dictates.

Bon appétit!

Introduction

Have you ever wanted to travel to other worlds?
Have you ever longed for helping companionship?
Have you ever searched for wisdom, clarity and direction?

These are the realms of the shamanic journey. It is in these realms that you will find your guides waiting patiently for you to ask them to take you places, to show you information and to gift you with power, energy and wisdom that can be used in your life here in the Earth realm.

Shamanic journeys are doorways to parallel realities. Within these worlds we find helping spirits capable of guiding us towards the goals or dreams we have for ourselves, personally and collectively. Shamanism is an ancient way of life, and yet we are seeing a great resurgence of it in today's mechanized world. Access to the world of spirit is simple and available to all; no high tech gadgets to buy, no professional degrees or years of study and expense needed. All that is required is the desire to move your life from where it is today, to where you dream it can be tomorrow and in the days and years ahead. The shamanic world will offer you information about existing dilemmas and show you new possibilities for living a more fulfilling life. It is not a world that dictates actions or absolutes, but rather a world that whispers possibilities of what you might do to solve these dilemmas. These whispers are then subject to your free will. All choices, decisions, and ultimately the actions to be done to achieve these goals are left up to you.

The Shamanic Journey is also a healing world. Entrance into the reality of disembodied spirit can help heal and soothe your mind, body and your personal spirit or soul. Sometimes a journey can be like a vacation from embodied life – leaving you refreshed, invigorated and ready to continue your path. The wisdom and direction found within a journey can both clarify and fortify your chosen path in life.

In following the shamanic path, you will be asked to look deep into your core being. In this core, you will find profound understanding and a deep love for yourself. At the same time you will gain an experiential knowledge of the connectedness of All. It is one thing to know that we are all connected, and quite another to experience that connectedness. It is in this space of connectedness that we find the notion of shamanic ecstasy – oneness with all our relations, embodied and disembodied, with Creator/source, with the All. Once you have experienced this ecstasy of connectedness and oneness, you will never feel alone.

When examining your core being, you will come face to face with aspects that are causing dis-ease, imbalance or dis-harmony within yourself. And what you find may not be easy for you to see. Shamanism is a very personal form of spirituality. You will stand naked before yourself and see yourself for who you are. You may learn things that you do not wish to learn; things that the spirits, who will guide you, know you must see if you wish to move forward to the person you desire to be. If you want to fulfill your intended dream, harsh as it may seem, you must see these naked truths. But as you listen to the words spirit gently whispers to you, you will soon feel within your heart and know within your mind the true nature of spirit Herself: love, understanding and compassion. The messages and lessons spirit will offer will always be laced with these three attributes. Fear not when you journey because you will never be alone. Always, spirit guides will be with you, whether those you work with on a regular basis or those who present themselves for the purpose at hand. Even when you are unaware of the presence of guides, they will still be there for you, for all that happens within the realm of spirit is ruled by those who dwell there.

A word about spirit guides

One of the most pleasant surprises to new journeyers is that these guides are true friends. They each have their own distinct personalities. Some are hilariously funny, some are coy, some tricksters, some pushy – and all are waiting to be asked to become an integral part of your life. Like all relationships, these relationships will need work so trust can develop in both directions. As in everyday reality, the relationships you have with spirit will change over time. New guides will appear and old guides may fall away for a time, only to reappear when needed.

By looking into this book, you have demonstrated the desire to explore the shamanic world in order to better yourself, and to better your relations with others, individually and communally, locally, nationally and globally. This is the all-important first step, your desire, your dream, your intent for a future different from the past. For intent is everything in shamanism.

There are hundreds of shamanic books on the shelves. Therefore, and rightly so, you might ask, 'What is so special about this book?'

We said shamanism is a personal journey, and it is. This is a book of shamanic journeys. As you will read in the first section, the shamanic journey is a way to access the world of spirit. Within this book you will find journeys that can help you on your personal quest to find the healing, wisdom and direction you both desire and deserve. What you do with the information retrieved from your journeys will be left up to you. We have grouped journeys with similar intent; however, you will find that these journeys can be modified for other purposes as needed.

Through the years both Eve and Robert have heard the frustration voiced by students of shamanism that it is often difficult or expensive to find shamanic workshops close to home, or to find trustworthy shamanic teachers with whom to study. Many people also tell us that they are able to begin their studies within the context of a workshop community, but then return home wondering what they should do next. This text will assist those of you who are learning on your own with the help of your spirit guides, and will provide continued study for those who have begun the path. It is for beginners and for seasoned practitioners. It is for healers who wish to introduce shamanic healing into their practice. It is, by nature, a self guided tour because the true teachers of shamanism lie within and around you. These teachers are your spirit guides emanating from your innate ability to connect with and relate to the spirit of the animals and plants around you on our beautiful mother – The Earth. Spirits of the Earth, of the Stars and of the vast cosmos. They are in Pachamama, all space, all time. The human teachers you encounter can only help facilitate your connection to spirit. This book will do just that – facilitate. It will give you suggestions for journeys that you can do as you exercise your shamanic muscles and open your imaginal mind to the endless journeys you can create on your own, and spirit will guide you on your path.

This is a reference book – a text book filled with ways you can approach spirit in order to find out how to move forward, to access inner healing power, to live complete and whole lives. It is written for you, the reader who holds a vision of who you want to be, who wants to co-create the community of your desire, who wants to to embody your dreams and to know your limitless connection. Or, as Ghandi put it so succinctly, who wants to 'Be the change you wish in the world'.

The Shamanic Journey

Shamanism is a term currently in use to describe traditions from geographically distant indigenous cultures with surprising similarities. These traditions are characterized by their life affirming ways, and by the honor and gratitude given to the natural forces of the physical world, our Mother Earth and Father Sky. There is a common experience of being able to communicate with the spirits and that by doing this we gain the knowledge that everything has spirit. Everything!

A good definition of a shaman is one who travels to alternate realities in order to bring back wisdom, energy and power to affect change in this physical reality. Within this definition are two essential key terms. The first is what this book is about – the altered state of the Journey – traveling to the alternate realities of the Spirit World - in what we will call journeytime (as opposed to what we will term everyday reality). The second is the distinction that the information, energy and power found in journeytime is brought back to Earth life in order to affect change in everyday reality. This differentiates the shamanic journey from other meditative altered states.

The journey is a basic tool used in the practice of shamanism. In the simplest terms, a shamanic journey is when the practitioner puts him or herself into a trance-like state and allows him or herself to travel freely through the imaginal mind, heart, soul and spirit. The level of trance is not important and may range from very light – like daydreaming – to very deep – like nighttime dreaming. The length of the journey is also unimportant and may take place in the space between two words – instantaneous – or may take hours out of everyday life. What makes journeying different from most other meditative states is the traveling, the receptiveness; welcoming in whatever comes and thus being transported to what is commonly called 'The

Spirit World', 'Otherworld' or 'Alternate Reality'. There, within that world and that reality, the mind can communicate with any and everything that presents itself. There, we find we are able to communicate freely and honestly from deep within our unconscious being, and in doing so we can access the collective unconscious. The person traveling on that journey then imagines, sees, intuits, or senses (in this text we will use the acronym ISIS) other beings with which he/she interacts. The object of the journey is to return to this world, this consciousness and this everyday reality, with knowledge, wisdom and personal power gleaned from the spirits living in that other journeytime reality, and to do so in order to effect a change for the betterment of the journeyer and/or for the local, national, global or cosmic communities – for all our relations.

Where is the journeyer to get the information, power and energy that we speak of?

From the journey itself, from alternate reality, from whatever the journeyer imagines, sees, intuits, or senses within the journey. In other words – from spirit.

What is spirit? We often banter the terms spirit and soul around without defining them, assuming that we are all talking about the same thing. It would take an entire book to explore these concepts. However, we will use the term spirit in the context of our text in journeytime as a disembodied entity. In journeytime spirit will connect with you and communicate with you in many ways, and may come to you in many forms. The spirit of the wind may come to you with the look and feel of a tornado, or a breeze, or may take a human or animal form. The connection and communication is what is important, not the form that the entity takes to come to you at any moment, which may change depending on what you are open to. In everyday reality, spirit is in everything. It is the force that animates virtually everything in the universe, including that which we term alive and not alive. Everything has spirit, and everything can be related to and communicated with.

Journeys begin with a release or relaxation to a different state of consciousness such that you are aware of spirit and are able to listen, to hear, and to answer. To connect and commune. To begin with this will be done in journeytime outside of everyday reality. Of course, with time, this may be a continuous or near continuous state of communion. The beginning journeyer, and even the most advanced journeyer, uses tools to focus the energies and for trance induction. These tools take different forms.

Traditional shamanic communities utilize what is present and available in their immediate environment as tools. We find shamanic tools very different in desert communities compared to those found in jungle communities. Working with the Shuar of the Upper Amazon of the Ecuadorian rainforest for over a decade, Eve knows the tools that this indigenous tribe use intimately. A Shuar shaman (Uwishin in Shuar) traditionally uses plant entheogens, specifically Ayahuasca (known as Natema in Shuar) to obtain a deep trance and the vision needed for the practice of shamanic healing. And yet a Shuar shaman, or indeed any Shuar living a traditional life, can go in and out of trance with ease without ingesting a thing. This is an important lesson that we need to understand when discussing shamanic tools. Tools are useful to focus our intent when communicating with spirit, but no tool is absolutely necessary.

Shamanic tools include drums, rattles, plant medicines, crystals, stones, fire, music, chanting, dancing, and many, many others.

The most common tool used to induce a shamanic trance for journeying in modern nontraditional cultures is the rhythmic beat of the drum (or rattle). This creates the same resonance as the Earth itself, and changes the brain waves (seen by EEG) to a sleeplike, dreamlike state. And yet, like hypnosis, you are not asleep. During a journey you are quite lucid, and most times are aware concurrently of the journey and of what is happening around you in everyday reality. Understanding this removes one of the blocks that people new to journeying have – that they expect a Technicolor Hollywood trip. These deeper journey states may or may not happen for you from time to time, but they are not necessary, universal, or even the most powerful in terms of what you bring back to affect change. When journeying (and perhaps also in life in general), simply open up to what is. Within 'what is' lies the map to finding out 'what may be'. This is why we say that whatever a journeyer imagines, sees, intuits or senses is valid. Many beginners only wish to 'see' their journey with visions. But using our other senses and our own innate intuition is just as valid and just as powerful in retrieving the wisdom, energy or power that a journey can provide.

Michael Harner is a much beloved teacher who created a system of shamanism which is outstanding in its reproducibility, teachability and effectiveness. Many of his first shamanic experiences were with the Shuar, and Harner graduates routinely use the drum and rattle to journey, at least in the beginning. It would surprise many of these fabulous practitioners that the Shuar rarely, if ever, use a drum. There are musical instruments among the Shuar, but the drum is not used in most healings or in ceremony. The Shuar drum is used most often to call a community together. In African, Native North American, European and Asian traditions, however, drums are frequently used to facilitate journeys.

In summary, the use of tools is a great way to begin to journey. With time and practice, however, these tools can be dropped as desired. We recommend beginning with drum, rattle, or even a drumming CD. It is, however, important with time to become proficient at communing with spirit and journeying wherever you find yourself and without a drum.

A word about time. Spirit time is very different from our sense of time in everyday reality. The Quechua know this, and for them the concept of time even in everyday life is time/space. Just as Einstein painstakingly proved mathematically many thousands of years after the Quechua cosmovision and language began, there is a space/time continuum. Everything that is, ever was, and ever will be. Not linear as we experience it without this language distinction. When we journey, this must be understood. Journey time is like a fabric and so the past, present and future are not always distinct from one another. They overlap as shamanic winds blow against the cloth causing it to fold over itself, creating points of connection. Perhaps because of this, questions about timing are ripe for miscommunication. There is a distinct benefit, however, to this time fluidity. A journey that usually takes you fifteen minutes to an hour to complete may, with practice or when in a pinch, be done in milliseconds of everyday time, retrieving the same information, power and energy needed for the intended change.

So how do you travel to alternate realities? What is this journey about which we write?

No one taught you to dream, and yet each and every night you know how to go to sleep. Dreaming comes effortlessly, with all its stories, messages and emotions. Lucid forms of dreaming, such as the shamanic journey, are just as natural to us and just as easy. We simply have not flexed this muscle or become conscious of its power because most of us do not live in a shamanic community. Worse than that, at an early age most of us were reprimanded for 'daydreaming' or for talking to 'imaginary friends'. These journeying muscles may have not only atrophied; they may have also been shamed out of us.

But they are still present and ready to be used.

In a shamanic community, like the Shuar, every morning the previous night's dreams are discussed by the whole family, and the significance of every minutia in the dream are interpreted to reap the messages. Even in daylight, with each decision, spirit is asked for assistance. Journeying and help from spirit guides are a part of everyday life and do not require practice. This is the traditional indigenous way, and looks very different from the path that urban nontraditional peoples use in order to reconnect, those described in this book.

An 'urban shaman', devoid of this communal support, must first come to the understanding that journeying is innate. With this understanding, you will come to know the supporting community of spirit. Following the journeys which call to you in this book, you will begin to regain the trusting relationship that you had with spirit when you were a child, and come to trust this community in your everyday life. With time, the journeying and connection with spirit that exists everywhere and at all times will become a way of life. It is then that the urban methods of shamanic practice will fall away and the traditional shamanic ways of your distant ancestors will come to life in you once again. Only then can we all walk in spirit together as indigenous peoples.

What we are trying to impress to you now at the beginning of this text, is that people have different ideas about how to approach shamanism. For an example, Eve who works with shamanic communities in remote areas, does not journey in the same way that Robert does, who lives and practises in the United States. The "urban", or perhaps more appropriately termed nontraditional, methods outlined here speak to peoples who have strengthened their mental capacities - those of us who live in industrialized nations. Beginning to connect with spirit where we are so very full, in our head and imagination, will then provide spirit access to our heart. This is our prayer for you. For as our hearts open more and more and strengthen, our whole being connects with spirit in a much more simple, open, traditional way. One that is unique to each of us. For we all walk in spirit with our unique perspective, and that unique connection is important to our global and universal community in life, to all our relations.

Similarly, shamanic teachers who reach out to industrialized peoples approach this task of reconnecting us to spirit in different ways. Some tend to give shamanism more structure than others. Some are adamant that a particular method for approaching the subject is the way it should always be done. Others say that whatever works for you, the shamanic practitioner, is the way it should be done. We suggest that whatever is in your heart is your truth. Throughout this text, we never expect you to do as we dictate. The journeys that you will find listed here are only suggestions, journeys we have done personally or have described to groups. After you have read the book, please accept only what you wish; discard what you choose and change any journey in order to mold it to your personal situation. If, while on a journey, your guide or intuition takes you in another direction, then by all means go. Your relationship with the spirits of non-ordinary reality will ultimately lead you in the direction that is in harmony with yourself, not us or anyone else. We believe that there are NO RULES for the shamanic journey.

Let us add the following for those of you who are truly beginning on the shamanic path. If you do not have the opportunity to attend workshops or otherwise find experienced shamanic practitioners to help you on your personal journey to change your life, it does not matter. There is nothing you cannot discover on your own as you begin your walk on the shamanic path. The true shaman or shamanic practitioner will tell you that the real teachers are not the people you encounter who know more than you do, but the spirits themselves. And everyone can encounter those spirits. All you need is one tool: trust. You MUST trust yourself, trust spirit and trust that the information you receive from spirit is true and valid for you in your life at the time of the journey. And know that your expectations and attachments to outcome can fool you as to what you are hearing. Learn discernment, and take the time and energy to build your relationship with spirit carefully, frequently and with commitment and honor. (Both Robert and Eve readily admit to never having been steered wrong by spirit, but also admit to steering themselves wrong at times that they failed to listen to spirit's call.)

The power behind shamans or healers is not intrinsic. No one shaman is truly any more powerful than another. All are equal in the eyes of spirit because a shaman's power does not lie within the person. It lies within Spirit – Pachamama, Mother Earth, Mother Time and Mother Universe. The power to listen, to hear, and to effect change does, however, lie in the depth of connection. This you can, and must, cultivate. (Note: This is not said to in any way detract from our elders and their extensive wisdom and power drawn from a lifetime of experience working with spirit, but rather to remind you to get out of your own way and let spirit work through you.) It is the spirits themselves who give you knowledge, energy and power and the trust we just spoke of to affect change. You must feel deep within your heart that the information you receive from the shamanic journey is true and valid, and learn to hear when you are to take action in everyday reality.

In the beginning, building that trust may be slow. But as you become more skilled in your journeying techniques, that trust will slowly grow and keep growing until your trust in spirit is complete. Because of this, and because it takes time to learn to discern our attachments from what we are hearing from spirit, begin with the intent to effect small changes and as you gain trust expand from there. With deep connection, there is no limit to the change that can be effected.

Will it happen? Yes.

How long will it take? It's impossible to tell. It may take time; it may wax and wane; it may be present already.

There is nothing mysterious or magical about journeying. A journey, for the purposes of this text, is nothing more than active dreaming, a daydream, something people do in all walks of life, in all economic conditions and in all countries of the world. If you have ever closed your eyes and imagined yourself someplace else, doing something different, or if you have ever gone on any imaginary trip to give your mind a break from the daily stresses we are all under, then you can journey. If you have ever meditated and in that meditation found something that you did not expect to find, you can journey. If you have ever done any creative imagining, then you have journeyed already

So how do you do it?

The easiest way to answer is: any way you wish. What follows below are some of the ways shamanic practitioners enter non-ordinary or spiritual reality – what we will call journeytime for the purpose of this book. As you read, if something strikes you in the moment as something that you feel you want to do, try it first. The opposite is also true. If something strikes a note of discord within you, then perhaps skip it. Of course, you could always mix and match, add from your own imagination and subtract what doesn't feel right to you in your heart. The important thing is not how you connect with spirit world. The important thing is to connect.

How to Start a Journey

Find a quiet space. You may want to lie down or sit. Dim the light; begin with eyes closed to avoid distraction; turn off phones, and maybe pop in a drumming CD especially made for journeying. Relax your mind and body. Uncross your arms and legs and take some deep breaths. Later you can drum or rattle for yourself, and eventually journey anywhere, anytime, without tools.

Beginning a Journey 1 - Safe Place:

This is a common method of entry and many people begin their journeys this way.

Imagine you are in a safe place. You can be anywhere – your house, your garden or a park, a make believe place or a place you have been to already. Bring to mind this place where you feel completely at ease. Imagine yourself really there. Try to use as many of your senses as you can – seeing it, hearing it (birds, insects, waves, wind, etc.), smelling it. Don't be discouraged if you cannot see this visually within your mind. People experience journeys – and gather information, power and energy – in different ways. We are visionaries, auditories, sensitives, empathics and intuitives. We are all of these, but each of us experience spirit more strongly in one or two ways, and that can change from journey to journey. Some see events unfolding one after the other as in movies. Some do not see anything but sense what is there. Others may just intuit the information. Some hear voices or words. Some experience emotional 'gut' feelings. If all else fails, begin by imagining it! All these experiences, imagining, seeing, intuiting and sensing (we use the acronym ISIS) are completely valid and no one method is better or worse than another. In the text we will tend to use visual terms to describe the journeys; however, remember to be open to whatever way the journey presents itself to you in the moment.

People often ask us, 'But how do I know if I am imagining the whole thing?' And we say, yes. Yes – especially to get things going. Where do you think imagination comes from? Some would say – from spirit.

So – to continue – from that safe place, imagine yourself covered by a white or silver light coming from Mother Earth, light that surrounds and protects you. The important thing for you to remember is that this is your place, a safe haven where nothing can harm you. From within your safe place, open your heart and call out for a spirit guide(s) to come to you. Imagine a guide coming toward you. This guide may appear in virtually any shape, though many experience their guides as animals. Spirit may come to you as a person, a ball of light, or a large tree that is in the middle of the path before you. Ask whatever spirit comes if it is your guide. The answer will come, perhaps as a voice – yours or another's – or as a knowing. If the answer is yes, converse with this guide and ask questions – you have begun your journey. If the answer is no, ask whatever spirit has come to you if he/she will take you to your guide. Either way, you will have begun your journey. You may have one guide that will always come, or many. Guides may change depending upon the intent of the journey – some guides seem to love to involve themselves in particular issues, perhaps love, or finances. You may find this is true for your guides, or it may seem that they randomly appear. One guide may shapeshift within a journey, or from journey to journey. Each guide has his/her own personality, sense of humor, insight and way of speaking and divulging information, wisdom and power. You will find that you develop relationships with different guides in very different ways. And some people do not work with guides at all, but simply call out to Spirit at large within the journey.

Beginning a Journey 2 - Lower World:

The next way to begin is a very classic way of journeying, especially as it is taught in the United States.

Imagine an entry into the earth. It can be a hole in the ground, a cave, a hole in a tree, the roots of a tree, a waterfall - anything that leads down. If it is a real place, fine. If not, also fine. Imagine yourself standing next to that opening. Now, enter it and descend into the earth – down, down, down. If you need to imagine yourself shrinking to the size of an ant to fit into the hole, then do so. Imagine, see, intuit or sense (ISIS) yourself flowing down through the earth. You may find yourself in a tunnel or cave; wherever you find yourself, travel to the end of it. You may find yourself coming out almost immediately or it may take you a little while. Each person experiences the beginning of a journey in a slightly different way. When you come out of the cave or break through to another place, you will be there, in spirit world. Call out and ask a guide to appear. Ask anything that you imagine, see, intuit or sense (ISIS) in the journey if it is your guide, or if it can take you to your guide. Ask a rock, a blade of grass, a tree, a river, a lake, the sky, the air; ask anything or just ask the nothing that you sense, for that nothing is part of spirit and also has a voice.

For those of us who live in urban environments, the opening leading into the earth could be a crack between the sidewalk, a staircase or escalator going down, the entrance to a subway (if your city has subways) or an elevator. If you use the elevator, imagine yourself pushing a button, SW for Spirit World, then imagine, see, intuit or sense (ISIS) the door closing and the elevator going down. When it stops and the door opens, you'll be there.

The entrance could be the stairs in your home that leads to the basement; it could be the entrance to the Holland Tunnel if you live in New York or a tunnel in your own city. Some people just imagine walking into their bathroom, flushing their toilet and riding the swirling water into the Spirit World. For those who have never tried this, the toilet that leads to the spirit world has never been used as a toilet, is always brand new and sparkling clean!

When he first tried journeying, Eve's five year old son saw himself in a mall. He described walking into a store that was empty except for a huge table in the middle. He climbed onto the table and there was a big hole which he jumped down. He found himself at the bottom in a forest where a video game character bounced up to him and invited him to climb on its back, taking him off on an adventure. So you see that these classic methods seem to be universally present in our subconscious, collectively, and that we find that they come to us without formal teaching in everyday reality, even if from a place as seemingly mundane as a mall.

Beginning a Journey 3 - Upper World:

This is the same as above, however find anything in journeytime that leads upwards. It could be the branches of a tree, the wind, a kite, an escalator... You get the picture. When you go to the Upper World, some find that they meet different guides there from those that you meet in Lower World. You may find that you are called to go up for certain intents and issues, down or middle for others. If you are not sure, ask. You can always go down if you are up, and up if you are down.

Beginning a Journey 4 - Middle World:

Imagine you are standing at the entrance to your living room. It is your living room and you know everything that is there without any effort. See the furniture, perhaps a pet that comes to greet you; notice whatever is there; imagine it. Now, imagine in the wall opposite you, a door that doesn't exist in everyday reality. See yourself walking to that door. Imagine yourself lifting your arm and turning the doorknob. Imagine, see, intuit or sense

(ISIS) your hand as it turns the knob. Open the door and step through it, knowing that when you cross the threshold, you will be where you are in the place you need to be to talk to spirit today for this journey, for this particular intent. Middle world is spirit world, and it looks like everyday reality.

Alternatively, when you open the door you may ask to be in nature. Wherever you find yourself, call out to spirit, ask for a guide, talk to what comes to you.

Beginning a Journey 5 - Nature:

'Be' in a forest. Imagine, see, intuit or sense (ISIS) the trees; listen to the leaves rustling in the wind; see the birds or hear the insects. Walk down a narrow path through the trees and imagine a clearing in the near distance. Within the clearing, imagine a rock. Go to the rock and sit on it, and then call out to spirit for a guide to come. You may imagine yourself on a beach, in a meadow, on a glacier. The where doesn't matter. Just open your heart and call out. And remember: imagine it happening, you being there. And if you call out as soon as you know you are in the forest or on the beach, before doing what we suggested, the shamanic police will not come to arrest you for doing it incorrectly. Whatever works for you is the way you should do it.

Finding Your Spirit Guide

If you already have spirit guide(s), move to the next section. Or you may take this journey to find more guides or to deepen your relationship with existing ones.

JOURNEY: Your intention is to meet your spirit guide and begin to establish a relationship with that guide in any way that feels right to you.

Begin with any of the ways from the previous chapter. When someone or something appears, begin to dialog.

Ask:

Q: Are you my guide? If not, please take me to my guide.

Once you meet your guide, ask whatever questions you feel are important, but remember that since this is your first journey, it is better to keep the questions simple.

We suggest:

Q: Why are you my guide?

Q: Why did you come to me today?

Q: What lessons do you bring me?

Q: What energy, information, power do you bring to me?

Q: What can you tell me/show me that I need to know in my life at this moment?

Of course, these are our questions. They are not yours. For all the journeys in this book, think of our questions as suggestions only. Question crafting is all-important, and if you get an answer that you do not understand, try clarifying the question. The questions that you feel in your heart are the ones that are the most important. (If you have any problem with this journey, you may wish to first try the journey 'Totem Animals' for additional understanding and help.)

Basic Principles of Journeying

Rule number 1 – There Are No Rules

Find a quiet space in your mind.

You may or may not be in quiet space externally.

You may or may not have a tool such as a drum or rattle.

Time is relative.

Open yourself to possibility and experience what is.

You can journey for yourself or for another, alone or in community.

Set your purpose for the journey clearly in your mind – your intent.

Clarify this intent before the journey. Clarification of your intent may itself require a journey with that purpose, or even a series of journeys to come to fruition, however, it is always worth the time and effort to do so. Clear intent will enable you to be sure that you shift in the direction that is in your and all your relations' highest good.

Put your hand on the steering wheel and BE the intended dream, that intent.

Craft questions carefully (rarely ask yes or no questions, they only give yes or no answers).

If you don't understand the answer, reword the question.

If your guide will not answer a question, you may not be ready for the answer. Try again another time.

You may ask for a guide to come to you and address questions to that guide. You may ask spirit in general. You may ask the spirit that is the image of the journey's intent (a problem, dream, dis-ease, element etc.).

Remember you can ask for help from anything and anyone that you sense in your journey.

Trust spirit.

Develop spiritual relationships with guides by acting on

advice, returning with gratitude, and asking for more information. This ongoing and mutual relationship builds trust, as in all relationships.

Go with the flow.

Gratitude, gratitude, gratitude.

In the alternate reality of journeytime, feel and experience the energy of your intended shift. Shifts that have a 'good' impact not only on you, but on all your relations and on our Earthly world, are always more charged and shift at a more rapid pace than more narrow and personal shifts. We put the word 'good' in quotation marks because, of course, this is a relative term. (In spirit world, we suggest you ask what the ramifications are of this shift as you hone your dream to one that feels right in your heart and soul, and one that feels aligned with your community and with all your relations.)

Be that energy – never wish to become that energy, just BE.

Remember to stay in a state of compassion for self and others.

Remember to thank your guides before you end each journey.

All outcomes are a gift with information, energy and power, even unexpected or undesired scenarios which can help you to hone intent.

Spirit will give you exactly what you need, not what you want. Be with what is in journeytime and not with what you wish it to be.

You will find a way that works for you to begin your journeys. Many journeyers begin in a safe place, or go into the Earth through a hole or the roots of a tree. There is no right way, and even when you find what works for you, you may decide to change this method at any time.

You may find a guide, or guides, who will help you; or you may commune with spirit in general. You may journey with questions in mind, or simply to heal and bask in alternate reality.

You may feel spirit and alternate reality sensually – through vision, touch, smell, sound, taste – or you may simply have a knowing intuitively. There may be symbols that you tease the meaning out of, or volumes of information that seem to download instantly and then take years to articulate.

End each journey by bringing the energy, wisdom and power into your Earth body and feeling the influx of vitality.

There are no rules.

There are no rules.

You will learn what works for you. Some people need time to do all this and to let things sit and gel. People who access very visual story-like journeys full of symbols often like to journal their journeys. Those who receive a lot of instantaneous intuitive information may need time to be able to articulate everything into our non-spiritual language. No matter how you access information, try different ways to bring the energy, power and information into your body – journaling, dancing, music, painting, dialogue, running, being in nature, conversing with the trees and sky and stars and river… Find your own way to embody spirit.

Eventually, it would be ideal if journeying can become a constant state of being – walking between the worlds. This is a way of being more like that of indigenous peoples the world over, a life where each breath, step, bite, thought, word – everything – is spirit. Where there is no need to take time out of daily life to be still or to drum in order for a guide to answer questions and provide assistance. Where we are living each moment in right action, assisted by spirit, in harmony and deep connection with Mother Earth/Pachamama/space time, aligning the flow of the grand forces of nature/destiny with our free will.

Crafting Questions

Clear intent is crucial for the most productive journeys. Stating a clear intent sets the stage for the questions. Before the journey has begun, it is best if the journeyer knows what question or questions they wish answered. In many cases, the possible answers we could receive will have a direct relationship to how we phrase the questions we ask. You may ask, 'Should I take the new job?' However, you may get only a 'Yes' or 'No' answer rather then the information you need. 'What is it I am not seeing about this new job?' or 'How will it affect the people in my relationships?' are questions whose possible answers hold more information.

Wording is important. We said there are no rules; however, in regard to phrasing questions, there are some general guidelines we suggest you follow – at least in the beginning:

- Never ask a yes or no question because this sets extreme limits on the amount of information that you can receive.
- Never ask a question that you do not want the answer to.
- Try to state the question in a simple, clear sentence. That way, the answer you will receive MAY also be clear. The clearer you can be about the kind of information that you want from spirit, and the clearer your question, the easier you make it for spirit to answer you, and the easier it is for you to decipher their answer. If you do not get an answer, or if the answer you perceive is unclear, try rephrasing the question being more careful with your wording. If no answer comes after this, consider that you may not be ready for the answer.
- Listen to your heart. Chances are, you already know the answer.

There are times when being non-specific can be an advantage as well. Asking, 'Why is my supervisor always criticizing my work?' will give you specific information about the relationship between the two of you. But asking, 'What is the nature of the problem that exists between my supervisor and myself?' may allow a much better understanding of the dynamics occurring, not only in the office, but also in the supervisor's life. That information could be just as important to you. Try to phrase your question to get the most possible information from the answer.

After you become familiar with your various guides, you will intuitively know that certain guides will respond better to certain types of questions than others. Each guide has a personality, and over time we have found that, just as with human friends in everyday reality, our conversations differ with our different spirit friends. Conscious awareness of this will allow you to change the question from that which you originally planned to ask your guide, to one that fits the personality of the guide that shows up in your journey.

It is important to remember that many times our definition of a word may not be the same as spirit's understanding of it. Take 'time' as an example; asking spirit 'when' something will happen could provoke an answer of 'soon'. But to an ageless spirit, her soon and our soon can be separated by years! Knowing these limitations, you may want to just leave out the 'when' in a question. Even if you do get an answer, it may be very difficult to understand. With practice, you will find other words or phrases that your guide may avoid answering directly. Never push the guide to respond in a certain way. Either try the journey again later or rephrase the question in a way that will reveal the answer. Perhaps, instead of asking 'when' something will happen, you could ask 'will (it happen) this year, or by the next full moon, before or after I move (or something else happens)'. Yes, these are yes or no questions. Remember, even when we suggest something to you, the 'There are no rules' still applies.

Be prepared to ask your guide immediate follow-up questions; in the 'time' example, either leave timing out entirely, or bracketing a time between other events that spirit understands. In this case, yes or no questions may actually be the perfect ones to ask in narrowing down a time frame.

Play with wording and find out what works best for you. Think about the information that you wish to receive and then craft your questions carefully. Your goal is to adjust and clarify the question to get the most helpful information possible in the journey you are about to take. And when you have that clarity, begin your journey, letting go of all of your preconceived ideas of what the answer should be. Spirit often surprises us and instead of giving answers, gives us more question, more food for thought. Remember that spirit will give us the answer that we are ready for and need – not always the ones we feel we want.

The Journeys

The following journeys will provide you with ways to obtain from spirit all the knowledge, wisdom and power that you need to affect the change in your life that you seek. Each journey is a template. Try it and see what comes. You can begin in any way that feels right, and be open to what happens. The important thing is to begin. And if you ask us what will happen as you walk this shamanic path that you have chosen, we answer, 'Something wonderful!'

The Essence of Your Dream – Honing Intent

Intent is everything in shamanism. Remember the saying; be careful what you wish, for you just might get it! A great deal of time in shamanic practice is spent in learning to hone intent to its essence, teasing out the difference between the change we truly want to affect, from the symbol of that change. For an example, if you have the dream of winning the lottery, explore the essence of that dream. Is money just the symbol of your dream? What is the essence of the dream? To have the freedom to do your heart's work? To have the power to do something? To be able to support your family? To travel?

Statistics show that most lottery winners are very unhappy a few years later. In our experience, putting your energy into a symbolic fantasy such as this can divert you from the path of getting where you really want to go. Make sure you have clarified exactly what you wish to achieve. What is the essence of your goal, your dream, your intent?

This is the only rule – clarify your intention. It is arguably the most important, and difficult, step in shamanic practice, and we suggest that it is prudent that the intention of your first journey to be clarification of your overall intent - obtaining a clear picture of the essence of your dream/goal. (This journey is important before any of the other journeys in this book.)

JOURNEY: Your intention is to clarify your goal.

Begin the journey in your chosen manner and picture your dream/goal as if it has manifested already. Be with this new life and try to experience the energy associated with it. Not necessarily the details of this life and certainly not how you got there. Experience the energy of this manifested dream. How do you feel? Is there anything in this scenario that feels uncomfortable in journeytime? Does it feel good? Ask that future self, your guide, or ask spirit in general if the dream/goal you are sensing in journeytime is in your higher good? Ask how this will effect all your relations – your loved ones, your family, your friends and the world. Ask how it will affect you. Ask what the negative sides of 'being' your dream/goal are? If you imagine, see, intuit or sense (ISIS) that all is as it should be, then fine. You are clear about what goal you wish to achieve or what problem you wish to solve. But if you sense that something in your goal needs to be altered, then begin to hone the dream within the journey to the essence of that dream, of your chosen shapeshift, whether physically, situationally, emotionally, mentally, spiritually or communally. Alter the dream/goal and, if necessary, repeat the beginning of this journey and BE with THIS new life, asking the same questions, until you have a sense that your goal is clear. Then, and only then, you can BE the new dream in everyday life. BE the energy that is the essence of your goal. Feel the new you deeply. Take action. Ask your guide or spirit in general what the first step is in everyday reality that you can take to begin moving you forward into achieving your dream. Bring the energy of the dream that you experienced in journeytime frequently into your everyday life – again, not the details, but rather the feeling and the energy of the dream.

Totem Animals

Shamanic lore has spoken of these special spirit guides for millennia, depicted in the earliest human art forms in caves from as many as 70,000 years ago.

Even today, shamanic societies call upon their totem animals (also called power animals) for help and guidance. From an early age, children in shamanic cultures find which animals they have an affinity to, and discover which attributes of these totems they hold personally. Many times, totem animals will appear before us, often while we are asleep in dreamtime. In Western society where children's dreams and fantasies are not supported, and even discouraged as children grow older, we forget the earliest attempts our totem animals made to connect with us. Indeed, as we have said on numerous occasions to people just beginning to walk the shamanic path, learning how to journey and to connect with spirit is no more difficult than remembering our childhood dreams.

The vast majority of shamanic practitioners the world over have power animals. One animal spirit may be dominant throughout your life, your totem so to speak, and yet like other guides, totem animals may come and go. Some like to help with certain recurring tasks, and at any given moment you can journey to ask which animal spirit will answer your call for help.

Some people like to create and carry images of their animal guides to remind them to embody the spirit and essence that these spirit animals bring to us. Ask all your guides how they would like to be remembered, and honor them in whatever way they ask. When you are comfortable with your journeying skills and with your relationship with your totem animals, there is a journey you might like to try. Journey to each and ask permission to merge with them, becoming one with them, feeling their energy and life essences in journeytime spirit world. A wonderful way to honor your animal spirit guides is to dance them in everyday reality. As trance state occurs during the dance, journey to them and ask permission to merge energies, and then allow them to take over and dance you. This journey dance not only allows you to honor and to give gratitude to them, but also creates an opportunity to embody the power and energies that they bring to you into your physical form and into your life.

Once you have begun to embrace a shamanic way, animals may also come to you in your everyday reality, literally crossing your path, or grabbing your attention several times within a short time. Pay attention! This spirit guide is coming to you with a useful message, power and/or characteristic energy to help you in your life. What does this animal mean to you? What are its attributes? Are you able to see these attributes within yourself? Can you express these attributes more? Do you see a need to embody these attributes at this time in your life? What does this animal bring to you? Journey and ask.

We would like to remind you that when you ask for a guide, even if you are expecting an animal, it may also come as a plant, a color, a stone or any other object, or appear to you in any way the guide chooses. Be open to inviting in the power, energy and wisdom of whatever comes to you at any given time, either in journeytime or in your everyday life. Some people believe that these lifetime occurrences are just coincidences, but shamanic tradition embraces the idea of synchronicity and that these 'coincidences' happen for a reason.

At this point, you know that you can experience a journey in several ways. From now on, we are going to use the word ISIS as a mnemonic to simply remind you that however you perceive the journey is exactly the way it should be in the moment, the way spirit is choosing to communicate and connect with you. ISIS is the perfect mnemonic for shamanic journeys as she is the ancient Egyptian Goddess of nature and magic. The mnemonic, as used here, stands for: IMAGINE, SEE, INTUIT or SENSE – ISIS. You may experience any or all of these in any particular journey and there is no preferred best way. There is only what is. Trust that the method(s) of perception that occurs in any journey is the best one(s) for you in that moment.

JOURNEY: Your intention is to find your totem animal and begin to build a relationship with him/her/it.

Begin as you wish. Ask your guides/spirit for help. When you find yourself in spirit world, ISIS your totem animal coming to you. Trust that first impression, that first thought or glimpse of the totem approaching you. Or from the beginning, ask your totem animal to join you somewhere in spirit world. Where are you? Look and move around. When an animal comes, ask if it is your totem animal guide. If not, ask it to take you to your totem animal. If you sense a 'yes', begin to get to know this spirit guide. Observe it. Feel its energy and essence. Ask questions. Some suggested questions are:

Q: What do you bring me?
Q: Why have you come to me today?
Q: What in my life needs your help at this moment?
Q: What lessons do you have to teach me?
Q: What in my essence mirrors your essence?
Q: What in my essence needs your essence?
Q: What attributes of yours would be helpful to bring into my everyday life?
Q: May I call on you in the future?
Q: How can I best honor you in my everyday life?

Take as much time as you need and do as many journeys as necessary.

Discovering the Root of a Problem

Most people can identify a problem that they feel is a priority to tackle; a problem that they believe they need to solve in order to heal and to find balance and connection. That problem, they feel, if solved, could finally help in fulfilling their dream/goal. What they may not be able to identify consciously is the root of this problem – a pattern of behavior, story or misconception; an event in their past; a stuck feeling, soul loss or other root issues.

Over the years that we have practiced shamanic healing, most of the people who come to us have in mind one identifiable problem that they wish to begin to solve. They think of this problem as that which causes them to behave in certain ways. They think that these ways of behaving have become habitual. By seeking help in discovering the root of the problem, they have admitted to themselves that these behavioral patterns no longer serve their higher good and need to be changed. By using shamanic journeying, the path to changing these behavioral patterns, no matter how ingrained, becomes much more clear and easier to follow.

The following series of journeys, done at whatever speed is comfortable for you, are designed to help you understand the problem you are working with by defining its root cause. Spirit will give you suggestions as to how you can begin to shift into the person you wish to be, and to manifest whatever dream that you envision.

As with everything else in this book, please take what you need and what resonates within you, and discard the rest. Once you understand the intent of your journey, modify or change the journey as you see fit, and of course always be open to spirit's modifications once you are in altered state. Remember, we only facilitate. Spirit is your teacher.

We will describe the journey using 'shyness' as an example for the 'problem' that you wish to work on.

One last thing before we begin the journeywork. If we were to say to you 'You say you realize that being ... shy ... is no longer in your best interest. So why don't you just stop? Go ask that person you like out for coffee; schedule that job interview you have been putting off, etc., would you answer, 'Because that's the way I am. I have always been shy and there is nothing I can do about it.' Our experience has been that this statement is NOT true, and that as long as you believe it, nothing will change. Although we all have a unique essence, what we do with this develops through our experiences. In other words, our behavior is a result of the choices that we made in our distant past and choices we continue to make in the present. You were not born with repetitive and ingrained behavior patterns; rather, at some point in your life, you chose to behave in this way. These journeys are designed to let you know why you made the choices you did. Knowledge is power. Understanding why you behave as you do is the first step in changing into who you wish to be.

JOURNEY: Your intention is to find the root of your problem – how your problem began and how you nourished it.

Begin this journey in your chosen way and when you find your guide, state your intention. Alternatively, state your intention to spirit in general: 'I wish to go to the place where (...my problem) began'.

Here is an example of how this journey might proceed. (As stated above, for the purpose of description in this example the problem being explored is shyness. In your journey, substitute whatever issue you wish to resolve.)

Imagine yourself moving from your safe place to a place in nature where trees or other plants grow. Once there, tell your guide or call out to Spirit (in altered state, not out loud) 'I wish to see who planted the seed that grew into my shyness.' You will now begin to ISIS (imagine, see, intuit or sense) a person coming and planting a seed in the ground. That person may be you as a child or even as an infant. But it doesn't have to be you at all. When you know who planted the seed, have a dialog with that spirit person and ask, 'Why are you planting this seed? What is occurring in my life that is making this necessary?' After asking the questions, you may hear the answer in words or not, but you will know the answer. You can then continue to dialog with the spirit of yourself as a child, or with whoever is planting the seed. Through this dialog, you may just sense or intuit answers; you may hear the dialog; you may even imagine the whole thing, but when the journey is over, you will come back to everyday reality with that knowledge.

After you know why the seed is being planted, watch/sense the person leave. Now, call out again or ask your guide the following: 'Show me who watered and nurtured this seed?' Again, a person will come to tend the growing tree or plant, watering it, feeding it, weeding the ground around it. It may be an older former self, but it might not. It might be a parent, a teacher, even a person you only met a few times in your life. Ask the same question to the spirit of that person. 'Why are you nurturing this seed? What is occurring in my life that is making this necessary?' You may find out what was happening in your past that reinforced your problem. Remember that this is a spirit who has come to help you. Ask questions and listen so that you may hear with gratitude and compassion. Repeat this process until you ISIS (imagine, see, intuit or sense) yourself as you are today. When you are finished, thank your guide. If you had no guide in this journey, thank spirit just as you called your intention out to spirit in the beginning of the journey.

After the journey, once you are fully rooted in everyday reality, write down all the information you can remember. Journeys often have a sleep-dream quality and some of us tend to forget them. Writing them down is a good habit to get into if you are one of those who forget, especially for those visionaries who get very visual and often symbolic dreamlike information that may require sifting through to interpret the symbols.

Before your next journey, think about what occurred, and feel the emotions that are involved. Think about the root of your shyness and how it has been nourished and perpetuated. Think of all the times you have been, in this example, shy, and ask yourself if, in each instance, you reacted in a shy manner because of the situation at hand, or because of what occurred at the root time. Let the emotions wash through you. There is no need to do anything yet. This is just a time to reflect and absorb the information and energy from the journey. Our hope is that you can understand on a visceral level, deep within your soul's being, the possibility that the problem you are dealing with began because it suited you, because it protected you in the past. That at some time, perhaps even as an infant or child, you chose that path. You chose TO BE shy. Now, however, as an adult in your current situation, shyness no longer serves you. Now you are asking for a change, for a new way of being. The next time you find yourself acting shy, choose to act in the moment. Be fully present while choosing your actions, rather than acting from past expectations. In this way you can choose to ACT rather than REACT. You can shift your way of being. You do not need to act according to past choices, and your current choices are not predicated by past events. You don't have to do anything yet except for being aware of what transpired in journeytime. If you can do that, you have passed a major hurdle in overcoming what is keeping you from your dream for yourself, your life and your community.

This is an example journey, and of course your journey will play out in a manner unique to you. Remember that in all journeys you may begin with any number of ways. Find your choice. You may also interact with any number of guides, or with spirit in general. It should also be noted that as the journey unfolds, you can interact with virtually everything that comes to you, whether in human form, animal, objects, colors, concepts, etc. Finally, find the ending that works best for you, giving thanks as always.

When you feel ready, you may move on to the next step: defining and breaking through the barriers that are preventing you from moving your dream life forward.

Discovering Personal Barriers

In order to begin your personal transformation, it is important to set your intent/goal/dream, and then simply be that. Not become – BE. Sounds easy? Then why do you find it so hard to shift into that new you? Why can't you change?

After honing your dream and exploring the dream's energy fully, you will encounter the barriers that have kept you in your current energy. That energy is what you must change, for it is no longer part of your dream – no longer in your higher good. Here are a series of journeys to help identify and break through the barriers to living the life of your dreams.

Just knowing why you persist in repeating a behavioral pattern (discovering the root of a problem) is usually not enough to alter that behavior. Knowing the root cause of why you act in a certain way can help, and yet a lasting change can often only occur if you, from the depths of your true being, wish to do the work that must be done in order for the change to take place, for the new you to take root. No one will do it for you. What is important to understand is that although the old energy patterns have been ingrained in you, you were likely not born with them. You may have been this way for a long time, and with each new situation, no matter how much you wished to act differently, something always stopped you. These are the barriers that you must begin to tear down in order to rid yourself of nonproductive behavior patterns. And it may not be easy. Barriers often have deep foundations and many people find it easier to chip away at these foundations, taking little steps at a time. Others may choose to tear them down at one setting using all their strength. As you proceed with the following journeys, you will soon intuit the best way for you to begin your transformation, your way of shifting into the new you.

JOURNEY: Your intention is to ask your guide or spirit to show you what your life would be like if you were no longer (we will continue to use the same example) shy. Again, of course, substitute your own issue.

What are the barriers to shifting to your new way of being, the barriers to dropping old behavior patterns, in this example, shyness. What stops you from being confident? The first journey to identifying barriers is to feel yourself already shifted, already living your new dream, and ISIS (imagine, see, intuit, or sense) how your life would be different if you were not shy. Journey to a life filled with confidence. Stay in your journey; experience and feel what your life would be like if you were not shy (or whatever issue you are working on). Feel the energy that is associated with that new life, with that state of being. While in this energetic state of not being shy in journeytime, specific barriers may readily come to you as you experience the journey. If so, acknowledge these barriers, talk to them, and ask their assistance. Alternatively ask your guide to assist you with these barriers. The next journey will identify more barriers that may be present, so do not be concerned if barriers are not apparent yet. While you are in journeytime, immerse yourself in this energy of Being Your Dream because then, when you return to everyday reality, you can recall the sensation of being in that energy until it is well rooted and you can fully BE it. (The old 'fake it till you make it' comes from this idea of being your dream until it takes root). The next time you must act in a different way in order to implement change in your life, recalling this energy will help you BE confident, not shy, in everyday reality. Consciously feeling this energy in everyday physical reality will help you recall the information, the energy and the power you received in your journey state and help you to change your behavior. It will remind you that you have been this way (confident) already – and are simply shifting energetically – moving into your dream into your new state of being; living your dream and co-creating it moment by moment, action by action, choice by choice in everyday reality. The next journey can be done separately, or you may simply continue with the questions from this journey.

JOURNEY: Your intention is to dialog with your future self in order to learn what specific barriers you need to dissolve to begin your transformation.

Begin as you choose. Ask your guide or spirit to take you to your future self after that self has removed the barriers to confidence (of course, substitute the issue you are working on).

You have experienced this confident 'future self' already in journeytime and have immersed yourself in that energy. Now, with intent, journey to that future self and dialog with it. First, explain who you are because that self is YOU in the future and deserves to know who you are now. For clarity in describing the journey, we will call this self 'Future'. Explain why you have sought out Future, and tell Future of your desire to finally rid yourself of the problem (shyness in this example). Ask Future what barriers it overcame so that it could make the shift into being that new person, the person you wish to be? Ask your guide or spirit to show you the first barrier you can work on breaking down. There are certain barriers that are universal and may well come to you. Some of these more universal barriers that we have worked with in the past include fear, denial of what is, jealousy and envy, attachment, doubt, and inertia. And of course some barriers are specific to your unique life and situation. Give yourself as much time as you need to complete this journey and ask any other questions you are called to ask. When you are finished, thank Future; ask for permission to return again when you need more help, thank your spirit guide and return from journeytime to everyday reality.

Once the barriers are identified, you may want to live with that information for a while. Think about the barriers; put them into some sort of priority list. Which one do you think you need to break through first, or do several have to come down at once? As you contemplate these barriers, do any other barriers come to mind? If so, add them to your priority list as well. Again, be open to spirit time and to the possibility that the barriers will timelessly breakthrough, opening you to being your dream. If you still feel that you are not beginning your transformation, work with the barriers; journey to them and ask why they cling to you and what you must do in our reality to begin to release their energy back into the Universal flow. Sometimes, only one or two need to be addressed in journeytime, and once momentum is gained the others fall away. Keep going back to the energy of Future in everyday reality as well, and BE the new dream.

JOURNEY: Your intention is to dialog with your barriers.

Begin as you choose. Ask your guide(s) or spirit in general to show you the barrier(s) to being, in this example, confident.

Talk to the barrier that comes to you. The easiest way to accomplish this in journeytime is to ask the barrier to appear before you in some form. It does not matter what form the shape takes, whether human in appearance or not. Dialog with that form, speaking to the barrier spirit that comes before you. A good way for you to end each dialog with the various barriers would be something like, 'Thank you for protecting me in the past and keeping me safe, but now I no longer need the protection you provided because it no longer serves my higher self. I'm asking you to leave and return to the Universal Energy'.

If you feel the need for more barrier journey work, read the journeys given below and select one. As always, you may create your own journey when you are clear on your intent. For the next journey select the barrier that you have decided is the most important one to break through and begin with that.

JOURNEY: Your intention is to journey to your Future self again and ask how he/she broke through the barrier(s) – both generally for all barriers, and specifically for each barrier in question. Be open to the wisdom and energy that comes. If emotions come, remember that these are energy as well and hold much information. You can ask the spirit of the emotion questions as well if that feels right to you in the moment. Or it may feel right to simply let these unblocked energies flow through you in journeytime so you can move forward.

Begin as you choose and, as in the last journey, return to your future self (Future). It is possible that Future may appear to you older or younger than the last time. That doesn't matter. If it is not the same Future, introduce yourself again and explain the reason for your visit. Ask Future self:

Q: Show me the first three steps I must take in my reality to break through this (name the barrier).

Alternatively, instead of going back to your future self, simply asking your spirit guide the same question works just as well. It is important to craft your questions carefully, and remember that if you don't understand the answer, you may not have asked a clear question.

When you complete the journey, you should know what actions you can begin to take in everyday reality in order to break through these barriers. If you feel the need to make these shifts slowly, when you have completed the first three steps, you may repeat the journey and ask for the next three steps to take in everyday reality, though many people intuitively know how to continue once they have begun their transformation.

JOURNEY: The intention is the same as above – to find out how to break through barriers. (This is just a different way for getting the information. The difference is in which spirit entity is called upon for answers, the spirit of the issue or the spirit of the barrier. Try them and find which method works best for you.)

In the beginning of your journey, either while you are still in your safe place or before you call for your guide, imagine that the problem (the shyness in this example) has a physical shape. Again, what that shape looks like doesn't matter. Once you identify the shape, ask your guide (or spirit in general) to take you to the spirit shape (we will call the spirit shape in this example Shyness). Dialog with it. ISIS this shape and begin to have a conversation with it. Thank Shyness for being with you all these years and for the lessons that it has brought you, as well as for the protection. Explain that it no longer serves your higher good. Explain that the reasons it came to you in the first place are no longer valid. Pose the same question you asked Future to the spirit of the issue itself. You could phrase it something like:

> Q: Shyness, show me the first three steps I must accomplish in order for me to continue my life without you.
> In journeytime, everything can shapeshift with ease, so you might also phrase it:
> Q: Can you shapeshift from shyness to confidence? If yes, after Shyness shifts into 'Confidence', dialog with the new confident spirit form and ask:
> Q: How can I support your existence in my everyday life? If no, ask Shyness:
> Q: What can I do in everyday life that will support you and allow you to shift into 'Confidence'?

Once you have begun these steps, repeat the journey.

Regardless of which journey or journeys you have done to identify your barriers and how you have learned from spirit to begin to disassemble them, once you have returned to everyday reality your real work begins. You must put the information you came back with into action and begin to use that information to change your behavioral patterns. Two of our most beloved teachers, Ipupiara Makunaiman and Claicha Toocano, indigenous shamans from Brazil and Peru, have always said, 'All change comes from within.' And they are right. If you want to become the person you dream of becoming, you must first change within, and only then will you be able to take the steps in everyday life that will shift you into BEing that person.

JOURNEY: Your intention is to break down the barriers in the spirit world of journeytime.

Begin as you choose. Ask your barrier(s) to come to you and note the shape it takes. You may ask a guide(s) to assist you at any time if you wish. Depending on the form it takes, you are now able to dismantle, explode, melt or otherwise breakdown the spirit of the barrier. Alternatively, you could reshape the barrier into something that feels like an ally. If you choose this last option, a question you might ask the barrier is:

Q: How can we accommodate each other?
Q: What must I do in order for you to remain with the new me as an ally?

It is impossible to tell how long it will take for you to begin to see a difference in your life, but if you really want to change and are willing to do the work, the change will occur. When you feel that the process of change is well on its way, if you feel the need, then journey again to ask for the next three steps of breaking through the barrier. Alternatively, if these steps are sufficient for this barrier, and you are still feeling the need for assistance in Being (confident) – ask for information about breaking down the next barrier related to this problem. The process repeats itself until enough of the barriers have been broken down that you can see that you are BEING the person you wish to be. The repetitive behavior patterns that continually reinforced the problem will be altered. At this point, if you wish, you can repeat the entire process with a different problem.

What is important to remember is this: barriers do not just

appear. People do not just wake up one morning and decide they are afraid of dogs. Barriers are formed by life events and by the meaning you place on those events. The likelihood is that a person's barriers were formed and continue to thrive because they act as a self-regulator – a safety valve – to protect the person (i.e. never pet a dog – never get bitten). Also we are the ones who created our barriers and so we are the only ones who can remove them. Their removal can be instantaneous for some; however, for others, it can be a long and painful process, one filled with many tiny steps forward and what seems like giant steps backwards. But with time and effort, the tiny forward steps become larger and the large backward ones become smaller. Though many deeply ingrained patterns must be dealt with in this way, stay open to the possibility – to the magic and ease that can be found when working with the aid of spirit - the possibility that you will be one whose patterns shift immediately.

If you find yourself over time, perhaps at times of challenge, shifting back to your old patterns, repeat the process and ask spirit for help.

One last note: Suppose, after reading the above few pages, you close the book and say, 'This is nonsense. How can I close my eyes, imagine I go back into my past and find out something I didn't know that will help me solve my shyness right now? This whole thing is ridiculous!'

Our answer is to you is this: Whether the information you returned with is accurate or not, truth or truth highly embellished by your imagination or your conscious will to solve your problem, doesn't matter. If you act on the information as if it was accurate, positive changes will occur in your life. Your goal is to move into a state where you can begin the process of reshaping your life. If the goal is met – and it will be – then you and the shamanic experience will have succeeded! Remember, if the shamanic journey was solely an imaginary trip that had no effect in everyday reality, shamans and shamanic practitioners would not have been doing this for thousands and thousands of years. Do the work. Trust yourself. Trust Spirit.

Shapeshifting

Ancient shamanic stories tell us many tales of shapeshifting. In Celtic lore we find Druids changing shape from humans to oak trees, salmon and birds, while hags put on 'the glam' to appear as seductive maidens. Even in modern times, we hear of Amazonian shamans changing into jaguars, snakes, bats and other objects.

What is shapeshifting? In its simplest form, it is changing shape.

And what is shape? Shape is a pattern of energy. Change the energy and you change the shape.

In our culture, we have a hard time wrapping our brains around a change in physical shape. And yet this is part of everyday life. We began as an egg and sperm, and have shapeshifted into our current shape. The early shapeshifting changes are rapid and dramatic. Ask any mother of the miracle of birth, and the rapidity with which their newborn changes day by day.

The oats eaten for breakfast and carrots eaten last night are now me. Wow! What a shapeshift – a carrot becoming part of a human being!

When we gain or lose weight, become ill, become well, grow hair and nails, we ARE shapeshifting.

We can and do shapeshift energetically in subtle ways also, such as when we become depressed or manic, enthusiastic or apathetic. Ironically, our culture is more comfortable with the more subtle shifts like these – easing anxiety, dropping addictions and losing obsessions – than with energetic shifts that create physical changes.

We can also shift communally. Notice the changing values of the people who have adopted a Green Earth philosophy of life and have altered the lifestyles of millions of people throughout the globe. And remember how dedicated people, without conventional weapons, brought about the fall of communism?

These are all shapeshifts!

To paraphrase John Perkins from his book, *Shapeshifting*, one can categorize shapeshifting into three types:

1. Physical
2. Emotional and mental
3. Institutional or communal

The first step in any shapeshift is to know your intended shift, the dream of the new you. Read the section on honing your dream to clarify your intent. The second step is to know your current energy pattern. The third is to familiarize yourself with the energy of your intended shift. The fourth is to understand and breakthrough the barriers to this shapeshift. There are journeys that can help you with these steps in the section, discovering personal barriers. Then you can move onto the next step – actually shifting energy, easing from one energy pattern to the next. The final, and perhaps most important step, is supporting this new energy pattern and thus helping to prevent a backwards slip to former energy patterns and shapes.

You might rightly point out that all the previous journeys in this book are shapeshifts. And you would be correct. In this section we will describe a series of journeys for any intended shift. There is much overlap with other sections in the book. As always, choose your intent carefully. You might begin with something simple like a minor mental attitude change, or you can plunge ahead into shapeshifting major changes in your body and life. The intent of the journey is up to you.

JOURNEY: Your intention is to experience the energy of your intended shift.

Begin as you choose. Ask your guides/spirit to help you. ISIS the shapeshift you are intending to move into, as if the change has already occurred. 'BE' that new energy in journeytime, even if the intent is not a major shift. From within the journey, FEEL the energy associated with that new you. Sense it, watch it, be it and ask that shifted energy pattern in front of you whatever questions you need to ask. Spend as much time as necessary getting to know the feel of this energy pattern. When you feel that pattern deeply within you, go to the next journey. You may wish to repeat this journey more than once before moving on.

JOURNEY: Your intention is to find and breakthrough any barriers to the shift.

Begin as you wish. Ask your guides/spirit for help. ISIS (imagine, see, intuit, sense) yourself shifted again. Feel the shift deeply within yourself. ISIS any barriers to the shift. Ask your guides to point them out if need be. Be aware that some of the possible barriers to shifting include denial about your current energy pattern and situation, fear, jealousy, attachment to outcome, doubt in your ability to make the shift and inertia (wanting everything to stay the same). Another obstacle may be a misguided belief in a hierarchy of energy patterns. How can you make the shift into a bat if you think that being a bat is beneath you? You may feel that in this example you would be sliding down some illusory ladder of importance. You may think, 'What if I become stuck and cannot shift back?' Alternatively, you may feel you are not worthy to experience this shapeshift. Ask your guides for help with these barriers, and remember this: we are all one with everything around us. We share the same space, the energy, and the same place in the heart of Mother Earth. We are equal – we are all one. Can you ISIS any losses that you might suffer with this shift? Does any uncomfortable power or joy come to mind? If so, explore them, and decide if you need to hone your intent further. You may be surprised when you find that the barriers before you are not always negative. Often our greatest fear is to fully embody our authentic power. This book of journeys will help you to discover and to move into that power. Ask your guides/spirit to help you break through the barriers you found. Reread the journeys given before in discovering and breaking down personal barriers if you need to. And remember, breaking through barriers may be done in one or in a series of journeys.

JOURNEY: Your intention is to Shapeshift.

Begin as you wish. Ask your guides/spirit for help. Feel your current energy pattern. This is, of course, not static, and yet it has a definite pattern. Feel it deeply and know it. With intent, ease yourself fully into the new pattern, the one that you came to know in the previous journeys above. Physically, mentally, emotionally and spiritually, transform the old energy into the new. Spend time in this pattern to help it gel. Again, this may take one or several journeys to accomplish. For an example, if you are shifting into a snake, you may feel a need to express your shift through movement. If so, get up (or as a snake maybe slither on the ground), and with eyes half closed and still connected to alternate reality, dance your shift. Play with it; be with it – 'BE' it.

You may well ask, 'Why would I want to be a snake?' and we would ask in return: regardless of how you feel about snakes, are there any qualities which snakes possess that could help you in your life? A boa will wrap itself round something and cling tenaciously to it no matter what tries to take it away. A rattlesnake will back off if at all possible, but then strikes rapidly and effectively when it is important for it to do so. A king snake is harmless, yet in resembling a deadly coral snake it may avoid dangerous confrontation. And don't forget, all snakes undergo a deep purging through the cyclical shedding of their skin, ridding themselves of the old in order to make room for the new. What about bats, moles, rivers or volcanoes? If you could shift into their energy and claim it for yourself, would you find that authentic personal power we just spoke of? Would it amplify the power you already feel within yourself? Would this energy grow and become a major force in helping you move your life in the way you envision it? Ask your guides what shapeshift you need in your life right now. You may be surprised by their answer. All shifts will bring you deeper into who you are, even when what you find out is a resistance to the energetic shift. That is the power of shapeshifting! Knowing yourself, your own energy patterns, ever more profoundly.

JOURNEY: Your intention is to create support to the new shift.

Whether physical, emotional/mental or communal, we all need support to help us from slipping back into habitual energy patterns. There are many ways to support the shift. One is to fill your physical environment with reminders of your new energy.

When the Tibetans fled from the advancing Chinese, they did not grab the gold or jewels or other possessions conventional wisdom would say they take; they grabbed their thangkas (beautiful wall hangings with spiritual images) and their spiritual objects. In exile, these material reminders of their spiritual life allowed them to maintain their internal energy and to help support them in being Tibetan – communally and individually – the essence of their highest dream. This external support for internal essence is key.

One Buddhist belief is that a gentle soul born to aggressive, fighting parents will become angrier. And an angry soul born to loving, nurturing parents will become gentler.

Our environment helps to create our energy patterns. To the extent that we are in control of our environment and of creating the energy that we want ourselves surrounded with externally, we can support our internal environment energetically.

Begin as you wish. Ask your guides/spirit to help. ISIS yourself or your community already shifted. What images come to you? Be aware of all your senses within the journey: sounds, music, words, colors, textures, tastes and smells. When ready, ask to be shown a symbol or logo that embodies the essence of your shift. That symbol could be anything – a geometric shape, an object, an animal - ask whatever comes to you if it is the symbol. BE with it for a while. Merge with it, if you wish. Then, from within your journey, visit all the places that you go to in your everyday life in a typical week (home, office, favorite movie theaters or restaurants, and so on) and place that logo at each place in journeytime. When you come back to everyday reality, draw or find a picture of the symbol if you can. Perhaps it is a color, a sound, a taste, a texture, or a motion. Whatever it is, bring it into your daily life physically to remind you of this energy, and to support you in maintaining your dreamed of shift. Perhaps you can buy or make a little carving of your symbol and carry it with you to physically remind you of the energy that you have become, to remind you of your shapeshift. The next time you are sitting in your office and that annoying co-worker begins pushing your buttons; by looking at the walls with half-closed eyes and a little ISIS, you'll see your logo and breathe in the energy of the new shifted you.

Ask your guides/spirit what other ways you can support this new shifted energy within everyday reality.

When the journey is over, create this supportive environment - where you live and work, in your car, on your computer - everywhere. Surround yourself with this external support for your internal and external shapeshift.

The Elements – Claiming Personal Power and Wisdom

When we think of power, many of us define it as force or strength. By this definition, a lion is more powerful than a mole. But in spirit world, size really doesn't matter. Power is often more related to knowledge than to force, and the spirit lion and the spirit mole are equally powerful. For an example, a lion can teach you about patience when stalking a goal and how it is important to wait for the right opportunity to arise before taking action to bring this goal into your life. On the other hand, a mole may teach you about seeing in the dark with your inner sight, about the need for thoughtful actions, and the need to search out what lies unseen in the world, and in yourself. Both are equally powerful spirit allies; so welcome whichever spirit that comes to you. If you are a beginning journeyer, avoid the trap of wishing that a lion comes in journeytime to help you rather than a mole.

There are many ways we can go to spirit and ask for both knowledge and personal power to help us as we move towards our goals. What follows is just one. Remember that the hallmark of a shamanic journey, as opposed to other meditative states, is that you bring back energy, power and knowledge to affect change in everyday reality.

Perhaps you think that knowledge is more important to obtain for your life than brute strength, but know that strength can manifest in many ways. Inner strength is of utmost importance when making the changes necessary to achieve a goal, and in allowing the new information obtained in journeytime to come to fruition in your everyday life. For an example, it is not easy to change life long behavioral patterns and we can use all the inner strength we can get. Combining knowledge with power, however, creates the necessary conditions for change. And bringing in the energy of that change will manifest the shapeshift in our everyday world. In journeytime, if you seek information to bring clarity about an issue and, at the same time, ask for inner strength and power, you will have the tools you need to move forward. You may be more aware of receiving wisdom rather than power, or energy and strength rather than information, or all three equally. Trust that you will receive what you need, and repeat the journey as you feel called to do so. And when you are feeling a need for both knowledge and strength, we suggest that you try seeking out the spirits of the elements.

Earth, air, fire, water – the four elements most commonly described in shamanic communities around the world. (Note: Some traditions describe other elements such as metal and wood, or even others. Many consider these combinations of the basic four. Trust what comes to you. The intellectual descriptions are not important; the spirit that comes to you is.) Why seek an Elemental Earth Spirit? Each element is an ageless building block of who we are – of this Earth realm we call life. They are wise elders of the highest order. Each is filled with the attributes of love, understanding and compassion. All life on our planet is dependent on the energy each provides. But more importantly, each element's strength can be measured on a continuum ranging from absolute power and strength to the gentlest of whispers. This, coupled with the knowledge of how you might best be served by using these attributes in your current life, make elements perfect allies.

To demonstrate this, become still, close your eyes and bring in one of the elements. Let us use the element of Water as an example. The power inherent within this elemental spirit is unsurpassed. The tsunami in Asia several years ago changed the shape of the land, destroyed the human structures, and killed over 200,000 people. Each year, in countries all over the globe, as rain falls and rivers swell, floodwaters surge onto the land. Those waters can bring about death, disease and major financial losses. The surge of water that precedes a hurricane can wash away all but the strongest buildings. The Grand Canyon's creator was water. True, it took the Colorado River millions of years to shape the landscape, but the river was relentless and the end result is awesome! Yet, on a hot summer's day, a gentle mountain stream can refresh the thirsty traveler. The underground spring that finds it way to the surface can keep an African watering hole from drying out in the heat of the Savannah providing hosts of animals and people with life giving water without which they would surely perish. And who has not daydreamed of sitting by the shore of a gently lapping lake on a hot summer day? Water can be terribly destructive and marvelously constructive.

Each element has these seemingly paradoxical attributes. Our point is that within each element is a complex power of creative and destructive opposites that can be called upon. Filled with compassion of the ages, the elemental spirits can help support and rebuild us, as well as assist us in tearing down whatever is getting in our way of being the person we intend to be. They hold limitless knowledge of manifestation - after all it is an elemental world that we walk in.

In journeytime, you may also encounter a great spirit in shamanic cosmologies, the union of all the elements. This powerful union is universal, yet the word used to describe it varies throughout the world. Himalayan traditions know this as Ether or Consciousness and great Tibetan structures called Chortens (or Stupas in Sanskrit) are commemorated to the four elements and the fifth – the union of the four. The Andean Quechua know this union of elements as Ushai and call upon this power in the healing of people and of the Earth. Many traditions understand this union of the elements as spirit itself, and as the spark that brings matter to life.

JOURNEY: Your intention is to journey to the elemental spirits for cleansing.

This is a simple yet powerfully productive journey that can be done in just a few seconds, perhaps while brushing your teeth in the morning every day, or if you can give it more time, it can be like taking a long energy bath.

Begin as you choose. Ask the elements to come to you for cleansing. ISIS what shows up and relax into the journey. You may be washed in a waterfall or a gently falling rain. You may explode within a volcano or warm yourself by the embers of a fire. You may swirl upwards in a tornado or feel gentle breezes caressing your face. You may be covered in an earthquake's landslide or slip and slide in the mud. One or all elements may come to you. You get the point. There is nothing for you to do except experience the 'what is' in your journey. There are no questions to ask unless you wish to. Relax, soak it in, cleanse, heal, and recharge.

JOURNEY: Your intention is to seek out an element and ask what attributes of that element can best serve you now in your life.

Begin as you choose. Though you may be tempted to go to one particular element that you have an affinity for, it is best to ask your guide or spirit to take you to whatever element can best help you in the present. Just know that if you seek out Fire and a mountain appears, stay with Mountain. And if more than one elemental spirit comes, trust that this is what you need at this moment in your life. Remember to ask questions if you have an issue and if it feels important to you in the moment, or simply relax into the journey and let it flow, literally.

Allow your mind to ISIS (imagine, see, intuit, sense) yourself moving out from your safe place or wherever you begin your journey into space until the spirit of the element becomes apparent. It is always best to avoid having preconceived ideas about how spirit will appear. Yes, Water may be an ocean, lake, or river, but it doesn't have to be. Spirits can take any shape they wish and many times take the shape that will help us the most. If you encounter an unexpected scenario and are not sure which element is before you, ask from within the journey, 'Are you the spirit of...' or, 'What element are you the spirit of?' And if the answer is 'I am not an element at all', as always, go with it. Ask questions and see what spirit has come to you to and why.

Once you encounter the helping spirit, these are some of the questions you may wish to ask:

Q: Which attributes do you possess that can best help me at this time in my life?
Q: Why are these attributes important to me?
Q: How can I use these attributes now in my life, or in dealing with (state your issue)?
Q: What can I do to bring the energy of these attributes into my life?

Remember in past journeys how important it was to familiarize yourself with the energy, and to feel it deeply in order to be able to recall it and draw power from it in our everyday world? The same is true in this journey. As you dialog with the element(s), take a deep breath and breathe the element's energy into your body for healing, cleansing, breaking through blocks, and for taking in this power and energy bodily while you gain the wisdom needed. Ask permission to merge with it, become one with the element. In this way, not only can you breathe in the energy, you will 'be' the energy.

Other questions:

Q: What do I need to understand in dealing with (state your issue)?
Q: Why are you the element best suited to help me now?
Q: What do you bring to my family, my community and me?
Q: What obstacles may present themselves in everyday life as I embody your attributes in my life, or as I use your attributes to help me deal with (state your issue)?

Q: How can I best overcome those obstacles?

Q: Can you show me my life as it will be after I have dealt with (state your issue); after I have shifted into the me I intend to become?

Now, allow your mind to travel where the elemental spirit leads you. ISIS that future. Feel the energy of that future and remember it when you return to everyday reality.

Please note: the above may or may not be one single journey. Give it the time needed, and return as your heart and soul wishes, or when spirit calls.

Ancient Wisdom for Modern Problems

There are times for all of us when we find difficultly in coming up with a solution to a problem that has arisen for us or for our communities. We may find that sometimes this is due to our inability to look at the problem objectively, to see it within the context of larger issues. Has anyone ever said to you, 'Look at the big picture.'? This journey is about seeing things from a broader perspective.

When a situation comes up that requires some sort of a answer from us, human nature may lead us to believe that we are always right. The problem with thinking ourselves always right is that we view everyone who doesn't agree with us as always wrong. And we are never always right, just like we are never always wrong. Being able to look at problems and possible solutions objectively is an important tool. So how can we use journeytime to seek help from a wise spirit whose advice we can trust? Our suggestion is to journey to the Ancestors.

When a shaman or shamanic practitioner refers to the Ancestors, they may be referring to more than their family lineage, the people from whom they are directly descended. Although Ancestors do include your bloodline, they include so much more. Ancestors refer to those who have gone before us. Having time to reflect about their existence long after they have passed on, they have gained a body of collective wisdom that they are willing to share with us. And Ancestors do not have to be human. When journeying to the Ancestors you may meet an old tree, a mountain or an ocean that can count its memories in eons. Imagine the wisdom stored within the spirit of that ancient being!

JOURNEY: Your intention is to journey to an Ancestor and ask for knowledge or wisdom in order to deal with your current problem.

Begin as you choose, calling out your intention to spirit or your guide(s). In this journey, allow whatever you ISIS to take a life of its own and go with the scene that unfolds. There will come a point in the journey when you will find an Ancestor. This Ancestor may not always appear as you are expecting it to - as an elderly man with a white beard or a woman with silver hair. Accept and trust that who or whatever comes is exactly the spirit that has guidance for you today. An idea of some questions you might like to ask the Ancestor is:

Q: What is the nature of my problem?

Q: What is it that I am not seeing and what is preventing me from seeing it?

Q: How am I sabotaging myself?

Q: What part of me is resisting the solution of this problem, and why?

Q: What, if any, are the negative aspects of solving this problem?

Q: How can I solve the problem and remain in integrity, in harmony with myself as well as with the other people involved in the problem.

Dialog with the Ancestor just as you have dialoged with all the other spirits in journeytime. Don't forget to thank the Ancestor(s) before you leave, and ask if you can return if you need more information. Ask also if there is something you can do in everyday reality to honor those who have walked this Earth before us. And, of course, only ask this if you are willing to take whatever action is requested of you.

Is this the only reason you can journey to an Ancestor? Of course not. Remember, all the spirits in non-ordinary reality are willing to help us. Many times, they may shapeshift; change their shape without your knowledge. They will do whatever is necessary to feed us information in a way that is palatable to us. If your guide usually appears to you as an eagle but comes as a raccoon in order to teach you to mask yourself, then that is what your guide will do. Of course, it may be a different guide that comes, with a wholly different energy, personality and way of communicating and connecting with you. You may go to any spirit for any reason and find the answers you need. If you decided to go to an Ancestor and ask about your personality traits, you will get an answer that is just as valid as the answer you receive if you journey to the trait itself. But, the answer will come in a different form and may not give you as much information as you might get by getting to know the essence of that trait itself. As you get more experienced in journeying, you will find that it is easier to tailor your journey to your specific need at any time. If you are looking for wisdom about an issue, a journey to an Ancestor may be needed. If you are looking to overcome a fear of water, journeying to Dolphin, or even to the Ocean itself, might give you a better insight.

Who will ultimately decide who you journey to? Not us. Not even you. Spirit will. Spirit will always give you exactly what you need – not necessarily what you think you want. If you are journeying to Dolphin and you find that a dessert cactus is in your way, don't say to your guide or to the cactus, 'This isn't what I asked for!' Just ask Cactus if it is there for you, and if yes ask it whatever you wanted to ask Dolphin, and don't be surprised if it answers a totally different question, too. Be thankful, for the answer you receive is the answer you need most.

Dealing with Dis-ease

There are many success stories of people using journeys, oftentimes called guided imagery, to deal with dis-ease. This may be a diagnosed illness, or indeed any change that you wish to make in your life.

One example is the young boy with an inoperable brain tumor who would daily visualize the tumor and declare war on this place in his body by bombing it to shreds, as if his body were a video game. And the tumor shrank – much to the surprise of his doctors.

JOURNEY: Your intention is to create a change in yourself.

Begin as you choose. Ask your dis-ease to show itself to you. ISIS what it looks like? Examine it. Ask it questions. Ours might be:

Q: Why did you come into my life?
Q: What lessons did you bring for me to learn?
Q: Why have you decided to teach me these lessons in the form you have chosen? (Both the form you ISIS within the journey and the form the dis-ease has taken in everyday reality.)
Q: What must I do to have you leave me and reunite with the Universal energy?

Now ISIS this being, this dis-ease, changing into something beautiful – or if already beautiful, into something even more beautiful.

For an example, you may want to shrink a tumor, perhaps fibroids, or heal a wound such as an ulcer. Or maybe you want to lose weight or wish to enlist spirit's help in overcoming any unwanted condition.

Be open to the form that the spirit of the dis-ease takes in your journey and ISIS it carefully. If a lizard comes, is it large or small? What is its color, texture and smell? Speak to it. ISIS the lizard changing into a form that pleases you. Change its color, its shape, its size, etc. Don't like lizards? ISIS it shifting into a form you do like, perhaps a puppy, a kitten or another animal. If a stone comes, you could break it into pieces and create a mosaic, smooth and polish it into a beautiful shape, or cut it into a diamond. If a lump of clay comes, you may mold it into a magnificent statue. If a beautiful flower comes, perhaps see it growing into a whole field of flowers. Feel the energy of this newly shifted form. You get the idea. The point is to transform the dis-ease from the way it first appears into a pleasing, beautiful form, one that feels in harmony with you. Repeat this journey daily, or even several times a day, until you can just close your eyes and ISIS the new energy of the beautiful harmonious form, of the transformed dis-ease. Do this until the shift occurs in everyday reality.

Finding Harmony and Balance When You Lack Clarity

The shamanic journeys above, no matter how difficult they might have been to perform, were simple and direct in intent. You knew the problem that you wished to work on before you began the journey. You knew what aspect of yourself you wished to change and used the shamanic journey to begin your personal shapeshift. But what if you can't point to a specific problem? What if you just don't feel right or aren't content with the way your life is heading? What if you have lots of maybes in your head? What if you know you are not in harmony with your higher self, your relationships or the world around you? Always, always go to your guide and ask. It may take several journeys but eventually you will get all the answers you are ready for. Or you can take a walk in your spiritual garden as described in the journey below and ask the spirits you see there.

As we said before, it is a core shamanic belief that for every dis-ease in our reality, there is an equal and corresponding dis-ease in spiritual reality. As above so below, as below so above. If you are unhappy with any condition in our reality, that unhappiness can be seen in spiritual reality. If you journey to spirit world and ask to see the spiritual representation of your dis-ease, you will be able to connect directly with it. In this journey, you will not only find that dis-ease – you will heal it. Once the dis-ease is gone from the spirit world, then your healing in this world can move forward at a much more rapid pace. But don't forget, although the healing in this world can happen instantly, it usually happens over time as you embody the new energy, shifting and performing acts in this reality to support your new state of being.

Nan Moss and David Corbin, teachers for the Foundation for Shamanic Studies (www.shamanscircle.com) introduced Robert to their version of the following journey in their class, *After the Basic*, given at the New York Open Center. That workshop was a follow up to Michael Harner's, *Way of the Shaman*. Mr. Harner is the founder of the Foundation for Shamanic Studies (www.shamanism.org). Over the years, both Robert and Eve have been exposed to other variations of this journey, as well as leading their own versions of it. To repeat a theme already stated many times: what we write and how we suggest that journeys be performed are just that – suggestions. Mold this journey, like the others, to suit your needs.

The basis for this journey is the knowledge that for each of us there exists a spiritual garden, and what we find there is a reflection of where we are in our lives at the present moment. Our lives are in flux, and so is our garden. Journeying to your garden twice within a single week may result in completely different information. This journey will assess the 'now' in your life. Our spirit garden is a non-ordinary reality (another way of referring to the Journeytime, Otherworld, alternate reality, spiritual reality or spirit world) version of ourselves. Going to your garden is like a spiritual 'checkup.' Each time you visit it (and we suggest you do it regularly), we ask the spirit world, 'How are we doing?' If you are feeling disconnected from Mother Earth and everything around you, this journey is a wonderful way to begin to see what is wrong and how to rebuild and deepen those connections – to find harmony, balance and healing.

JOURNEY: Your intention is to find your garden within spirit world and begin working to make it harmonious and beautiful.

Begin your journey as you choose and then state your intention: 'I wish to be taken to my spiritual garden'. You will ISIS leaving your safe place, either alone or with a guide and find yourself coming into your garden.

At first, take time to look around (to ISIS around, but for sake of flow, we will assume that you know that the journey may or may not be visual at any time, and use sight to describe journeys). Take time to really 'be' in your garden using as many senses as you can. Begin your analysis with everything you ISIS. What does the soil look like? Is it rich and ready to nurture plants? What plants are there? Are they healthy? What colors do you sense are present? Are there weeds? Is there a water supply? Are there large rocks in the garden? Is there a bench or place to sit? Is there a shade tree? Is there a fence? Don't forget, these are our questions. Ask the questions you wish to ask as you take in the general appearance of your garden fully.

When you have a complete sense of what your garden looks and feels like, you can begin working in it. We cannot tell you what to do because every garden is different. This is your garden. But we can help you. Everything in your garden – rocks, soil, plants, weeds, bench, etc. – has a voice and all you have to do is ask. Then open yourself to hear, sense, imagine or intuit the answer. And keep asking.

For example, if there are a lot of rocks in the garden and those rocks are making it hard for the plants to grow, start removing the rocks. Each time you take a rock and place it outside the fence (or if no fence, outside the boundary of the garden), ask the rock, 'What in my present life do you represent and why are you in my garden?' This may bring awareness of reasons for the general dis-ease you are feeling. When the rocks are removed, continue working. If there are weeds growing, pull them up. As you do, ask each one why they are there. Thank them for wanting to help you with the lessons that they brought to teach you. Tell them it is time for them to return to the Universal Energy from which they were born. We have asked you to do this before, that is to thank spirit for hard lessons, and the reason is simple. It is better on a spiritual level to rid yourself of what no longer serves you from a place of love, kindness, compassion and understanding – no matter how hard the lesson was to learn – than from a place of anger and resentment. Pile the weeds outside the garden, and remember what they said to you. Everything you encounter in the garden holds information, energy and power for you.

What else might you consider doing?

- define the outside borders
- fix the fence
- till the soil
- remove large rocks or move them to create a path for you to walk along
- weed
- if plants and shrubs in are in pots, put them into the soil
- water
- trim plants and shrubs that are overgrown
- remove dead leaves or plants

As you remove each item continue to ask, 'What in my life do you represent?' Again, thank the dead plants or leaves for being in your life and teaching you the lessons that they brought to you. End the conversation by saying, 'It is time for me to move on with my life without you.'

Remember, each object in the garden represents a different aspect in your life, so ask the same questions to all the things you ISIS in your garden. Additional questions you might consider are:

Q: Why are you wilting?

Q: Why are you overgrown, under/over watered, broken or dying?

Q: What actions have I taken in the past week, month, year or years (ask whatever you feel is the correct question for you in the moment) that allowed you to reach this state?

Q: What is the first step or action that I can take in everyday reality that will support keeping you in a healthier and more balanced state?

Don't like these suggestions for tending your garden? You will know what is right – do those things. Remember, it is YOUR garden. Keep asking. Don't like our questions? Ask whatever you think is necessary. Trust. You'll know what to do and what to ask. Know that there is a direct relationship between the appearance of this garden and how you are living your life now, and to your current energy and state of being. Your intention for this journey is to clean up the garden so that you can find out about and begin to clean up the parts of your life that need to come into balance and harmony, to be beautified or purged. Most of the time, you will have a good idea as to how to proceed in everyday reality once the journey is complete. If you don't know, do another journey and ask your guide, what must I do in this reality to begin the change I started when I worked in my garden? You can also ask the individual items in your garden the same thing.

As described above, this can be a very long journey. You may wish to break it up into two or more. Use the first journey just to look at your garden, then in the second journey, return and begin working in it. After working on one or two things, you might end the journey and then return another time to continue.

The purpose of the 'Garden' journey is to obtain information as to why you do not feel content in your life at the moment; or why you feel out of balance; or why you are disconnected from your higher self; or why you feel disharmony in your relationships, or with the world around you. Armed with that information, you can begin to affect change in your everyday life.

Finding the True Source of Your Doubt or Hesitation

How many times in your life have you, after deciding on a course of action, procrastinated forever in carrying that action out - not only life changing actions like quitting a job before you find another, relocating to a new locale, asking your girlfriend to marry you and the like, but also procrastinating in doing the seemingly small tasks such as beginning to write that novel that is in your head, painting a room in your home, traveling, journeying to spirit, taking dance lessons, eating healthy foods, quitting smoking, or trying out a new activity with your friends?

In this journey, we hope you will discover the root cause that, over time, built the wall of procrastination within you. Just so we are all on the same page, we are not speaking about you not wanting to go to the store for a container of milk because it is raining; we are speaking about any activity that you have been putting off and later have asked yourself why. This wondering why wastes energy, and the resulting loss of vitality and frustration can be a cause of dis-ease both in spirit and within our physical reality. This journey is to prevent the dis-ease from concretizing in our lives and bodies by clearing the root cause spiritually. And the added bonus is that by dropping the procrastination in spirit world, when you are called to action in everyday world you will find it is much easier.

JOURNEY: Your intention is to find the nature of your doubt or hesitation in beginning or completing something you wish to do.

Begin as you choose. Ask to view or ISIS yourself beginning and/or completing the activity which you procrastinated in doing. Ask spirit to have all the obstacles, all the doubts, and all the hesitations take human or physical form in journeytime so that you can converse with them.

Now look for something within the journey that doesn't belong, or seems out of place. Ask this spirit if it is your procrastination block. If not, ask to be taken to your procrastination block. Confront the spirit of this block when you find it. A simple example follows:

> While journeying, you notice a strange dog sitting near you. That dog may represent something you should know. Ask if it is your block. If yes, ask if it will help you. Question this dog until you have discovered what you need to know about these blocks and how to open up your path. Our suggested questions are:
>
> Q: What are you preventing me from accomplishing?
> Q: Are you preventing me from accomplishing one specific task in my life or are you a major cause of all my doubts and hesitations?
> Q: When and why did you enter my life?
> Q: What purpose did you serve?
> Q: Do you continue to serve that purpose?
> Q: What lessons did you wish me to learn?

Ask for help. Ask the spirit form or your guide what your life would look like without this block or blocks, without your doubt or hesitation. ISIS that life and feel the energy associated with it. Ask what steps you can take in everyday reality to breakthrough the block.

Depending on what form these blocks take in journeytime, you may clear them while you are journeying. In this example, you could talk to the dog, lead it to the door, and send it home. Once the blockage is removed in journeytime reality, you may find it easier to begin to remove it from everyday reality.

Understanding Your Personality Parts

In this journey we are shifting our way of being in the world by shifting the patterns arising from our personality parts.

We are all filled with personality traits or parts that together make up our unique being. Eve often says 'it takes a village to be me', and by that she means that she is the product of a large group of personalities, archetypal and otherwise. When we say personality, we are not talking in psychological terms, although of course there is some overlap conceptually. Each personality part, from a shamanic point of view, is an entity with it's own desires, needs, and way of taking action. The parts may live harmoniously within you and with the world around you; however, there may be times when you feel out of balance. In this journey you will come to know the inner world of your personality parts and how these parts interact - with each other and with the outer world. This information will give you the opportunity to bring more balance and harmony into your life, and to find the most creative and productive way of being in the world.

Have you ever been annoyed with yourself for doing or saying something that, upon reflection, you would rather not have said or done? Have you felt that maybe your ego is too big or too small, that you are too quick tempered, or on the contrary that you never speak up for yourself, are overly jealous, too controlling or that you get lost in other people's decisions? Is it possible that you could be too aggressive or too passive, have trouble making decisions, or do you make hasty decisions and find later it would have been better if you had thought things through a bit more before taking action? Do you shrink from speaking out, or insist on being the one that is seen and heard over everyone else. Are you overly judgmental, or too forgiving in your life. Do you overspend like a jetsetter leaving yourself up to your ears in debt, or find yourself so thrifty that you feel uncomfortable every time a penny leaves your palm? Of course, we are talking about your own perspective, that is how you view your actions in your life, whether in retrospect or in the moment. Do you ever feel your repetitive way of acting in the world is counterproductive, gets you into trouble, or gets in the way of your dream for your life? Sound familiar? The following journey is especially useful if there is a part of yourself that behaves repeatedly in a way that makes you feel uncomfortable, or in a way that you think is not in your best interest. If you have ever said to yourself, 'I wish I hadn't done (or said) that', this journey will help you to understand yourself much better.

To give an example, imagine that lately you notice that you are getting into verbal fights with everyone around you – your spouse, family members, close friends and coworkers. You are aware of this pattern and feel uncomfortable with the way you are being in the world. You have promised yourself that you will stop but seem to be unable. In your journey, your goal would be to seek out – and give name – to that personality part of you responsible for this pattern. To meet the part that represents this way of being – striking out at people you care about – and dialog with it. You have already recognized that this part of you is not in harmony with the way you wish to be. By exploring this pattern in journeytime and gaining insight, knowledge and power, you can begin to take actions to alter that part of yourself, first in journeytime and then in everyday reality.

JOURNEY: Your intention is to dialog with the part of yourself you need to understand in order to shift your behavior to a more harmonious state – to shapeshift into the person you wish to be.

Begin as you choose. If you begin in a place of nature, start the journey from there. If not, we suggest you find a natural setting in journeytime where you feel completely at ease. Once there, try to 'be' in that place with all your senses; if the place is a beach, smell the salt air, feel the sea spray on your skin, hear the waves, feel the sand. The point is for you to be totally safe, secure and firmly planted in that safe space.

Now state your intention to your guide or just call out to spirit. Ask the personality trait that you wish to dialogue with to take a physical shape and come before you. Then, just wait. In a short time you will ISIS something or someone approaching. The form that the personality part takes in journeytime may give you information as to the way spirit, or your higher self, views that part, that aspect of your personality. Once you have a sense of the part in journeytime, invite this being to come and sit near you. Take in the energy and information that it is presenting with. Dialog with this spirit in order to get as much information as possible.

For an example, the personality trait may appear as a twenty-foot giant or as a tiny mouse. It may be a large, grotesque mass of junk or it may even be a whale that is able to walk on land. There is absolutely no way of knowing what will come to you. But whatever comes, remember that it is a part of you. Your goal is to talk to that part of you, to ask questions. What are some of the questions you might ask? Our ideas, not yours, include:

Q: Why are you coming to me in this shape and size? (Why are you this animal or person? Why are you a large jagged boulder?)

Q: What energy do you bring to me?

Q: What information do you have to tell me?

If an inanimate shape or object comes, get a sense of the texture and shape and ask:

Q: Why are you rough or smooth, curved or straight edged, hot or cold.

Get as much information as possible about this shape.

Next (and this is important) tell the spirit of the personality trait why you have called it to you, and state clearly that you would like to change that aspect of yourself and why. Then ask:

Q: What have I done in my life that made you into that shape?
Q: What do you look and feel like when in balance?
Q: How have I nurtured and supported you, or how have I ignored you?
Q: How have you nurtured and supported me?
Q: How have you protected me while becoming what you are today?
Q: What lessons did you want me to learn?
Q: What lessons have I learned?
Q: What lessons are you still wanting me to learn?
Q: What do you suggest I do to learn those lessons?
Q: How do you fit with the rest of my parts?
Q: How can I come into balance?

These last two questions are important as every part of you has a role, and if a part is out of balance it can create a great deal of difficulty for you in your life. For example, your inner judge has an important role for clear discernment and discrimination; however, when out of balance it can become judgmental and critical. Your inner warrior has a role to protect you and your loved ones, but out of balance can become angry and aggressive. Try bringing into balance your inner parent, your inner lover, wild one, student, teacher, child and many others. Ask your guide(s) which part needs balancing at this time, and how this will effect you as a whole.

After taking in all that the part has to say, you may negotiate with it in order that it becomes more compatible with your dream for your life. Tell the trait why you need it to change. Remind the trait that it and the other traits are in this together, one and the same, one within the other, and because of your present circumstances you, as a group of parts and as a whole being, need to come into harmony and balance in order to cocreate a new way of being in the world.

To return to the example of the angry fighting part of you, begin by thanking the trait for being a part of you, for protecting you all these years, for helping you and watching over you. Explain that you now find this protection overbearing (or not enough, depending on the trait) and counterproductive. Ask that part of your personality to reshape itself, remaining within you, but allowing you to move on with your life in a new way.

Tell the trait about the discomfort you feel with the way things are, and about the new 'you' you are shifting into. Recalling the physical appearance of the trait, tell it you wish it were smaller, bigger, smoother, rougher, warmer or colder. What you say depends on what you ISISed. Visualize the trait transforming its shape as you speak. Imagine it! ISIS it! Then ask these important questions:

Q: What must I do to support you in your new shape, to help you to stay in balance and harmony and to make you feel comfortable within the new me?

Q: How can we work together to create a better me, one that is in harmony and balance with those around me, with the world and with all of myself?

Q: What are you willing to give up to let me be the person I wish?

Q: What actions can I take in everyday reality for you to give this up?

Q: What must I do in everyday reality to accept what you wish to keep, and still move into the person I wish to become?

Q: What must I give up in order for you to allow me to move forward in my new life?

The idea for these questions is for you to understand what you can do so that you and the trait are balanced and harmonious, and that you as a whole can be productive in the world and in the life of your dreams. We outlined many questions here, and of course which questions you ask will depend on the information you glean from the part, from your guides, and from your inner instinct.

In any journey, you may find that the information comes nonverbally very quickly, and that you know exactly how to be in harmony and balance without much dialogue, or perhaps without any dialogue. If you find that you are gaining more information through questions, however, and that there is just too much information to ask and receive within one journey, break it up into two or more. Begin the second journey where you left off the first.

Ideally, after the conversation, you will ISIS your personality's shape change. When that change is complete, and before you return to everyday reality, thank the being that is the trait and watch it leave.

Why is this journey important for you? It will show you the true nature of the personality trait that you have called upon. You will see, in concrete form, what that part looks like. In most cases, if it bothered you enough to call it into your presence, you will not like what you imagine, see, intuit or sense (ISIS). You will then graphically understand the need to consciously rein that trait in at times when you find it ruling your actions. How you translate this change in everyday reality is up to you. If you need help at any time, either journey back to the trait or journey to your guide. Remember, your guide knows all the answers that will help you, but graphic representation and experiential knowing in journeytime help your guides to get these answers through to you.

If you promised to do something in journeytime to support the changes your part agreed to, you must carry them out. If they are difficult, take small steps, but begin taking those steps as soon as possible. Keep your agreements when conversing with spirit. That is how you begin to improve your relationship with spirit guides and how you build mutual trust.

Remember, the part is not your enemy. It is an integral part of you and has to remain so. When in balance, it is a very productive part of you. The example used above describes a personality part that needs to be reigned in, but you may find yourself journeying to an out of balance part that is weakened and needs to be brought out more. This is described further in the section 'Your Inner Warrior'. Also see 'Finding Your Shadow Self'.

Whether reigning in a trait or coaxing it out, consciousness and effort will be needed to continue the change you desire. We suggest you repeat this journey in 2 or 3 weeks, calling in the same part. At this time, you can again dialog with the part, noticing the changess in the part from when you first took the journey. This information will let you know if you are supporting it in the way you promised. If you are doing that, if you are working on changing who you are, then your life will begin to move in a new direction. If you are not, things will remain the same.

Repeat this journey as often as necessary, with any personality trait you wish to question or change.

One last point, in case it has escaped you up until now: All the journeys in this book are related and can be woven into each other. For example, after journeying to your personality trait, you could journey back to your garden with the intention of finding only those parts of the garden that are directly related to the personality trait. This will allow you to begin reshaping the spiritual part of your personality even before you begin to do the 'clean-up' in this reality. How you weave together the journeys in this book, and those that you and your guides create, is limitless.

Making Fear an Ally

In Understanding your Personality Parts, you asked the part to solidify and take a defined shape in journeytime. To come to you as a spirit entity. The reason we suggested this method is that the trait (shyness for example), is an abstract concept and having a conversation with the abstract can be difficult. Perceiving an issue in solid form moves it from the abstract to the concrete, to an entity that you can talk to and negotiate with. It is also our experience that this technique helps in understanding the issue or trait in its totality - it's essential energy, wisdom and power.

Journeying to an abstraction in physical form is a powerful way to affect change. This shamanic tool humanizes and de-demonizes an issue. It can allow you to view it from spirit's point of view. From that broader and higher perspective it may not appear as frightening or as looming as it appears to be in everyday reality.

In this section we will explore fear, a strong emotional energy that frequently and effectively blocks transformation. Can we reshape this energy and make it productive in our lives? How can you turn a fear (what you might think of as an enemy) into an ally?

Do you know how many people in our Western world will jump if a mouse runs across their path? A mouse cannot hurt you, and you know it. But will that stop you from jumping? Those of us who jump would have a very hard time explaining why. On some level, that fear is deep within us, unexplained and without logical cause in most cases. This can definitely work to the mouse's advantage. Suppose you could understand why you are afraid. Suppose you could find out what quality the mouse has that makes you jump. If you could erase your fear while taking in the energy of the fear so that it can serve you, it might work to YOUR advantage. To use the fear to prepare yourself to take the most productive action.

The first time that you try this journey, we suggest that you select something that is not a major fear. You can use a mouse if you wish to, or you can select anything else that frightens you. Don't make this a heavy journey at first. Pick a small fear, one that will allow you to test the waters and see how this shamanic tool can work for you. With practice, you can repeat it with stronger fears.

JOURNEY: Your intention is to journey to a fear and dialog with it.

Begin in your chosen way, keeping your intention within your mind and heart. Ask to be taken to whatever it is that you are afraid of. Be open, as always, to what comes. Ask questions. Take in the experience and ask your guide(s) to assist and protect you. If at any time you feel too anxious to continue, ask your guides to lift you away from what you fear until you can continue. You may need to do this several times, if necessary, until your anxiety lessens. If you feel too anxious at any time, you can thank that which you fear and come out of the journey. You can always return when you are ready to try again. Having said that, it has been our experience that if you ask for help, spirit and your guides will help you through this anxiety without a need to distance yourself. It may help, however, to keep in mind that you have that option. At this point in the journey there are two possibilities. You can communicate with the thing you are afraid of, or with fear itself, or both. Below we will describe the journey to fear itself, however you can substitute the object of your fear if this feels more appropriate for you in the moment.

Ask that the fear take a physical form (we will call it Fear). When you reach it, ISIS its shape, just like you did in previous journeys. Dialog with it. Feel the energy that emanates from this Fear being. Breathe it in. Claim it. If you can bring that energy into your life when there is a need, that fear will no longer be an enemy. It is our hope that when you return from your journey, you will be a little less afraid of this thing that you fear, a little wiser about its essence, its energetic properties, and about when you need those energies to support you in your life. At those moments that you need help in everyday reality, you can call on Fear and your guides to ask for help and advice. We are quite certain that if you do so, the spirit of Fear will be happy to help. Remember that spirit, even if it represents your deepest fear, holds the power of love, understanding and compassion.

Questions you may wish to ask are:

Q: Why am I afraid of this thing?
Q: What do I have to fear from it?
Q: What weakness, if any, within me is responsible for my fear of it?
Q: What is it that I do not know about it?
Q: What qualities are there in it that I am not afraid of?
Q: What about it is inherent in me?
Q: What does it bring to me?
Q: Where does it's strength lie?
Q: Where does your (Fear's) strength lie?
Q: How can I take in the energy of that strength and use it in my life?
Q: How can we accommodate each other so that I will not be anxious?

Are these too many questions for one journey? Perhaps. Should you do two journeys to the same fear? If you wish. Do you have to ask all of the questions? No. Which questions should you ask? The ones you want answered. Can you make up your own questions? You know the answer.

In fact, you know all the answers. Journey and this will become apparent.

Soul Hiding

This section was written with the knowledge, consent and help of Tom Cowan (www.riverdrum.com), a world renowned western shamanic practitioner, author of *Yearning for the Wind, Fire in the Head: Shamanism and the Celtic Spirit, Shamanism as a Spiritual Practice for Daily Life* and *The Way of the Saints: Prayers, Practices, and Meditation.* Tom has taught shamanic workshops throughout the United States and Europe and is recognized as a leading authority in Celtic Shamanism. Robert was introduced to the concept of soul hiding at one of Tom's workshops.

Soul Hiding is a technique that may allow you, as Tom says, 'to feel less vulnerable in a fearful situation and more in control or courageous about the action you wish to perform.' It involves asking your spirit guide to hide that part of your soul that feels open to attack, preventing you from accomplishing the task at hand.

Imagine you find communicating with your supervisor very difficult. You have requested an upcoming meeting with him/her and must be able to communicate clearly and efficiently in order to impress the need for a change in work rules, a raise, a concern about the direction of the company, something that is effecting office moral, anything that you have decided is important enough to ask for this meeting. But the thought of walking into the supervisor's office is causing a major upset within you. Soul hiding may be a wonderful remedy to the situation.

Please note: This journey requires the help of your spirit guide. Though most of the journeys suggested in this text are for both beginner and seasoned shamanic practitioner, beginners should not attempt this journey. Before trying it, you must have established a solid and trusting relationship with your guide. If you have any doubts, journey first and ask your guide.

JOURNEY: Your intention is to have your guide hide that part of your soul that feels vulnerable in your upcoming situation and preventing you from acting in the way you wish.

Before you start this journey, take either a clean palm size stone or a crystal and hold it in your hand, then start your journey as you usually do. When your guide appears, say 'I wish you to please hide that part of my soul that feels the most discomfort when I attempt to (add whatever you feel uncomfortable about).

You will then ISIS your guide doing what you asked. We have said before that in shamanism, there are no rules, and this holds true for this journey as well. There are many ways your guides can accomplish this task. Trust that you will know when the soul part has been hidden. When your spirit guide has completed the task, your journey is over. Before leaving your journey state, remember to thank your guide. Now, take the stone or crystal you have been holding and blow into it. The reason for this is, as Tom states, 'you are putting that part of yourself (the soul part being hidden) into the stone. Treat the stone as a container of your soul.' As you do this, concentrate on the task you wish to complete and know in your heart that spirit has completely supported you in your wish to hide your soul part.

Note: Keep the stone or crystal in a safe place. If you have an altar in your home, place your soul container on that. Or you may keep the stone with you as a huaca (pronounced wa-ka), Quechua for sacred power object. Either way, you will know that the hidden part of your soul is safe and secure.

The first time you do this journey, try it in a simple, relatively unimportant situation; try to find something small that you dislike doing or have difficulty in doing. An example might be having dinner with an over bearing in-law. Do the journey and then try to accomplish what you have been avoiding. See if you feel any differently inside. You may feel lighter and may intrinsically sense that the situation causing the difficultly is not as terrible as you felt it was before the soul hiding. Quoting Tom, 'The reason for this is that the energy you usually use to protect that part of your soul is now freed up to deal with the situation at hand. So soul hiding is actually a way to handle troublesome situations more effectively.' See if you can now accomplish the task. After you have the hang of it, try using this journey with other important tasks in your life that feel uncomfortable.

An essential part of the Soul Hiding journey comes after you have completed your task in everyday reality (made it through dinner without losing your temper, for example). You must ask your guide to return the hidden soul part. It would be presumptuous of us to assume that you can thrive without long term adverse effects with that part still hidden. You MUST reverse the process. Tom suggests that the reversal takes place within two or three days after you have completed the event.

The reversal is very simple and just the opposite of the soul hiding journey. When you are ready to do the journey, hold the stone or crystal and journey back to your guide. Your intention is to simply ask your guide to return your soul part to you. As with the first part of the journey, you should ISIS how your guide accomplishes this and trust that you will know when it is done. When the soul part is returned, your journey is over. Again, thank your guide before ending your journey. Since you placed that part of yourself into the stone in the first journey, reverse the process now by sucking that part back into you. Your soul will now be in the same state of completeness that it was in before your guide hid the soul part.

Sacrifice

The word sacrifice comes from the root sacred. To make something sacred we need to sacrifice something, often our attachment to ego or to a specific plan.

Sacrifice can mean different things to different people, and at different times. It may be doing something that you find very difficult. It may be giving up something that you value and are attached to. It may be letting go of a negative attribute that you cling to. All of these, however, are sacrifices and involve letting go of a part of you.

This is a simple journey that you can take in conjunction with any issue or journey suggested in this book. As we said in the introduction, all goals are set by you, and then all choices and decisions are up to you. And ultimately, the actions that are to be done to achieve these goals are also left up to you. If you listen hard enough, spirit will whisper to you, nudge you, or show you possibilities outside of those that you consciously hold in mind. Sometimes, spirit even gets your attention by pushing you hard. But spirit will not carry out the actions for you. If you do not take any action in everyday reality after a journey, then in all likelihood the issue will continue as if you had not journeyed at all.

There are very few people in this world that can have their way all the time. For the vast majority of us, life is a balancing act. We have to decide what we want, what we are willing to do to achieve it, and in many cases, what we are willing to give up in order to have it. It's the last one that gives us problems. Want that extra piece of delicious chocolate cake with the warm chocolate sauce that lies hidden in the middle just waiting to ooze on your plate as soon as the first prongs of the fork pierce the outer layer of the pastry? You can have it, but tomorrow you might have to spend an extra hour in the gym. That's the trade off. That's the balance many of us strive to keep in our lives. Always deciding, whether consciously or unconsciously, what we are willing to pay; what is the price of what we want and are we willing to pay it?

The great Sufi poet Hafiz tells it beautifully:

Manic Screaming
We should make all spiritual talk simple today
God is trying to sell you something but you don't want to buy
That is what your suffering is:
your fantastic haggling
your manic screaming
over
price.

When we ask spirit for help in solving an issue, most of the questions we ask revolve around our desires (what we wish to know, what we wish to accomplish, and how we can accomplish it). In the journey state, we rarely remember to inquire about the price. We usually fail to ask our guides, 'What is it going to cost me?' In many of the journeys in this book, we suggest questions as to what difficulties, if any, will occur if you affect the change in everyday reality. This implies that there is a personal cost, a sacrifice that will be required in order to shift your issue and to fulfill your dream. In this journey, we suggest that you focus solely on the price – on the sacrifice.

JOURNEY: Your intention is to ask your guide(s) or spirit what you must sacrifice in order to achieve your goal.

We told you that this is a simple journey and it may well be simple to perform; however, the information you cull from it may not be simple to put into action. Once you have connected with your guide or have left the security of your safe place by calling out your intention, there are several questions we suggest that you ask:

Q: What must I sacrifice in order to achieve my goal?
Q: Why must I sacrifice this in order to achieve my goal?
Q: What might prevent me from sacrificing this?
Q: What is the path of least resistance I should take in order to sacrifice what I must?
Q: What is the path of most resistance?
Q: Which path is in my higher good?
Q: How can I let go gracefully?
Q: What will my life look like after I have sacrificed this?
Q: How will it affect my relationships? My community?

We do remind you that this is a journey for knowledge. What you do with the information is entirely up to you. If, however, in journeytime you promise your guide or spirit that you will sacrifice something in everyday reality, we strongly suggest that you honor your word. And if you find that you spoke in the moment and need more time to fully commit, simply journey back to your guide(s) and discuss this, and if needed amend your agreement. Remember that spirit, encompassing all aspects of love, understanding and compassion, will fully support you in moving forward at your own pace. Well, at least sometimes.

Finding Your Shadow Self

Do you think something is missing within you but you're not sure what? In other words, you are generally content with your life and it is moving in the direction you wish. You have no pressing issues at the moment and perhaps you journeyed to your garden and found it in pretty good shape. But yet...

What is this something that you feel is missing? This nagging feeling? It is possible that there is a part of you that is hidden deep inside of you, and is longing to be heard. This journey is to explore that part of you that your higher self has sequestered deep in your unconsciousness. This is a journey to your Shadow Self. You are simply trying to discover parts of you that have been sequestered deep within you. You are doing this in order to assess whether bringing the energy of this part back, whether in it's current state or modified, will increase and round out your energy in everyday life.

The fun part about this journey is in being able to truly 'Be' that shadow self in journeytime, and in experiencing whatever worlds this journey reveals, and the stories that unfold. You may find yourself diving into archetypal energies and collective stories, or into deeply personal fantasies. This will not be a story that you wish to manifest in everyday reality. It is not generally a dream that you wish to come true. It is a fantasy, and as such – as you are not putting any energy or thoughts into having this story materialize in your everyday world – you can go deep and let the fantasy rip.

JOURNEY: Your intention is to view and merge with your shadow self, fully experiencing the fantasy that unfolds - only in journeytime.

This journey is in two parts. You may attach the second to the first and do it as one if you wish. The instructions for the first part are simple. Start as you choose and ask your guide(s) or spirit to take you to your shadow self. Once there, be with whatever you ISIS. In journeytime, merge with and become one with that part of you that is hidden away if you are able. In journeytime, spend a journey day with that shadow self. Feel the energy that is associated with that self and notice how that energy is different from your energy in everyday reality. Do you feel that this shadow energy might be part of what you thought of as missing in your life? Do you think that by consciously bringing some of this energy into your current life, you might find yourself more complete? There are no questions to ask your shadow self unless you feel you need to. There is no dialog to hold, unless you wish to. Just 'be' that other self.

Robert: 'When I did this journey, I found myself in the back of a large limousine. I was a mobster. There were several other people in the car and as I barked orders to them, they answered 'Yes Boss,' to each order. I was rich and powerful and not afraid to do whatever I had to in order to become richer and more powerful. I may be chagrinned to say so, but part of me enjoyed that feeling of absolute power over the people in my organization. Well, I don't know if I had an organization, but at least I controlled the people in the car.'

What do we want you to get from this journey? We wish you to come away knowing a side of you that you had no idea existed. We want you to try to understand your feelings towards that side of you. Do not censor this journey as if you were in everyday reality. Remember that it is a fantasy. We want you to fully be your shadow self. Then, we want you to do the second journey. (If you are doing this as one journey, ISIS yourself pulling away and leaving your shadow self. Call out this new intention as you leave.)

JOURNEY: Your intention is to ask your guide(s), an Ancestor, another spirit you have worked with, or just call out from within your journey, 'How can I bring the essential energy of my shadow self into my everyday reality in a way that is aligned with the higher good?'

In part one, you experienced a completely different life from the one you normally lead and, if you are like Robert, you may have even enjoyed it. But, that life is a fantasy. Although Robert felt through his shadow self the energy of a mobster, he didn't emerge from the first journey wishing to go into a store in everyday life and extort protection money from the owner. Whatever you experienced in the first part of your journey must remain totally within the realm of spirit. What is important is to deeply feel the energy associated with that shadow self. With Spirit's counsel, you will find a way to bring some of that positive energy into your life and to channel this energy in a way that supports your true dreams. This energy is missing in your life, hidden deep within you. Accessing this energy in journeytime and bringing it back can engender a sense of wholeness that was not present before you began these two journeys. This may be the reason that you felt the nagging sense of something missing; this may have been Spirit calling to you.

Is this shadow journey difficult? That depends on your shadow self. For an example, in Robert's second journey, the message he came away with was to be more aggressive.

Robert: 'After working on that issue for a while and doing some of the other journeys suggested in this text, I began to bring the 'mobster energy' into my life. I spoke up for myself when I felt I needed to, and not just with major issues. I did it because in order to be in harmony with the person I was trying to become, I needed to incorporate that shadow energy which I had experienced in my journey in my everyday life. After the journeys, if I felt the dry cleaning wasn't done properly, I brought it back and had them redo it rather then let it go like I used to do before bringing in this energy. When I had a minor problem with a credit card company, a store or the phone company, I didn't accept the customer service person's 'I'm sorry, there is nothing I can do.' I asked to speak to a supervisor. If the answer the supervisor gave was no, I accepted it. But many times, I was heard and listened to. Whether or not I got what I wanted was not the issue. Before bringing in that energy, unless I felt that something was important, I would let it go. I decided that the confrontation would be more difficult for me and, for an example, I could afford the 89 cents for the phone call I didn't make. By supporting my shadow self, by bringing that energy into my life, I began to speak up for myself, not just in large issues, but in the small ones too. I practiced incorporating that shadow self energy into my life in a good way.'

One last suggestion: Do not ask your shadow self how to bring the energy into your life. Ask your guide. This will help to ensure that you do not bring the fantasy into your everyday life, but the energy of your shadow self that is in your higher purpose.

Journeying to a part of you that you are unaware of can be a very useful tool on your shamanic path. Below, we are going to give you a few more intentions for similar journeys. Follow the same procedure; first 'be' with that part and then find a way to bring the energy into your everyday life. Or, as always, come up with your own journey to retrieve the information.

JOURNEY: Your intention is to ask your guide or call out to spirit to show you the inner child that is inside you and how to bring the qualities that are in the higher good of that child into your life.

JOURNEY: Your intention is to ask your guide(s) or spirit to show you the mother that resides within you and to bring that inner mother into your everyday life to hold you, nurture you and advise you.

JOURNEY: Your intention is to ask your guide or call to spirit to show you the masculine side of your personality if you are female, or the feminine side if you are male. Both energies, male and female, are within you. Denying one completely can cause dis-ease. This journey will allow you to get in touch with that other side and bring parts of that energy into your life now, achieving balance. You might wish to journey to the energy of the same sex that your body holds in this life. This energy may also need to be modified or amplified in your everyday life. You may be surprised by what you have hidden deep within. Also note that what conventional wisdom sees as feminine and masculine energy may not be what comes up for you in any given journey. To use Far Eastern terminology, energies include a yang yin and a yin yang, a yang yang and a yin yin. No matter how these energies present themselves to you in journeytime, and in everyday reality, be open to learning more about universal energies, and how you can use these energies in your life.

JOURNEY: Your intention is to journey to your inner judge. In experiencing the shadow side of judgment and taking on this energy, it may be possible to bring more discernment into your everyday life and drop the judgemental side, thus accessing your inner wise person.

Know that you may be taken to any shadow being when your intent is open-ended to spirit. You may also ask to be taken to any particular being, archetypal or otherwise, that you would like to be with in order to know this within yourself and to transmute it into accessible and productive energy, power and information. See if any of these call to you: try journeying to your inner king or queen, your inner joker, your inner saint, hermit, bagwoman or homeless person, your inner muse, visionary, warrior, lover, cripple, victim, perpetrator, matchmaker, prisoner, wild one, femme fatale, etc. You may also be taken to a person, historical or fictional, who holds certain archetypal energies in our collective mythology. To Buddha, or Mahatma Ghandi. To Ghengis Khan or Mother Theresa. To Jesus or any one of the Mary's. To Cinderella or the Wicked Witch of the West.

The only limit to what energies you access is your willingness to open yourself to them and to the flowering of spirit's direction through your intent.

Finding Your Inner Warrior

In Finding Your Shadow Self, we told you how the message came to Robert that he needed to be more aggressive. The question we pose now is how do you know when something is worth being aggressive about? We're not speaking about major issues like the bank misplacing your deposited paycheck. But how many times do we get into situations which we can either confront or back away from? How many times do people in your family, at work, your friends or others push the limits of your boundaries? Where do you draw the line? Should you spend three hours on the phone arguing with your local telephone company over an $0.89 charge for a long distance call they insist that you made when you know that you didn't? Economically, it's not worth the time and effort. But intrinsically, to support the person you wish to be as you travel this path, it may be very important. How can you find out when to put forth energy, and when to retreat? Journey to your inner warrior.

(Of course this journey can be modified for any of the shadow beings that you incorporated in the last section, not just the warrior).

Your inner warrior is just what the name implies; it is the spiritual representation of the warrior within you. Remember, we told you in the section about Ancestors that it is helpful to journey to the spirit guide who can give you the most direct information. If you have need to confront an issue that involves a possible struggle, the journey we suggest is to go to the spirit who knows your personal power better than anyone, including your conscious self – the spirit who has been with you since you were born and whose wisdom lies within the figurative field of battle.

JOURNEY: Your intention is to go to your inner warrior to find out if a particular 'battle' is worth fighting at this time in your life.

If you perceive that the answer is yes, your intention shifts to 'How can I prepare myself for battle, what 'weapons' do I need (information, situations, timing, place, etc.), and what actions must I take in everyday reality to be the most productive in the fight?'

If the answer is no, your intention becomes 'what must I do now? Am I to retreat in order to arm myself with the information, power or energy needed to return to the battle? Or am I to retreat from this 'battle' forever? What steps must I take in everyday reality to give up the 'battle' or 'war' and still be in harmony with myself and the world around me? What message(s) does this conflict hold for me?'

As with everything in spirit world, nothing is as simple as we have stated above. The first thing we have told you is to ask your inner warrior is a yes or no question. Never ask yes or no questions because all you will get is a yes or no answer. When we journey, most of the time we don't want these kinds of answers; we want information. Then why did we suggest you ask that? In order to get a yes or no answer that will direct the journey along one of two very different paths from the very beginning of the journey.

It is better not to have any preconceived notions about how your inner warrior will appear to you. It may be a Roman soldier ready for battle. It may able be a sloth moving ever so slowly down a tree.

In addition, whenever we give you the questions, you must decide in what order you wish to ask them. If you wish to take several journeys instead of one, please do so. Or if you can think of other journeys to gain as much information as you will need before confronting your son or daughter, husband, wife, coworkers, friends, the phone company, etc. do it your way. You might even journey to ask your guide to speak to their guides in journeytime. This can open up communication in everyday ordinary reality seemingly magically.

Here are the questions that we think are important:

Q: Are there any actions I can take in everyday reality that will settle the issue without it causing harm, without 'the fight?' If the answer is yes, ask:

Q: What are those actions and why must I take them? You should also ask some of the questions that are listed below even if you can avoid the struggle. Remember you are journeying to receive information, and you can get that by asking questions.

If the answer is no, continue with:

Q: What is the real cause or nature of the issue?

Q: What am I not seeing about the issue that I must see in order to be productive?

Q: How will my success in this 'fight' affect my life and the lives of the people I care about?

Q: How will my succeeding in this issue effect the people who did not succeed? What if, after you have asked this question, you ISIS something that makes you feel uncomfortable, that is not compatible with your higher good? For example, you sense your co-worker gets fired and that getting another job may be difficult, resulting in the loss of his/her home because he/she can't pay the mortgage. If what you ISISed does not sit well with you, ask:

Q: What actions must I take in everyday reality that are harmonious with my higher self and my community in order to succeed? If there are no actions, then ask:

Q: Is this battle worth the price that someone must pay if I succeed? (It may be that only you know if you are willing to pay the price, in which case you may get that answer, or you may get no answer at all.) If the answer is yes, ask:

Q: Why?

Q: What will be gained?

Q: What will be lost? And if no, return to the 'No' intention given above. (What steps must I take in everyday reality to give up the 'battle' or 'war' and still be in harmony with myself and the world around me?)

It's not simple, is it? Each question you ask may not be an end in itself but only lead you to other questions. The point is that the more information you have, the more possibilities your inner warrior has made you aware of, the better armed you will be when the time for action begins. Even though it is cliché, this is the second time we have said that Knowledge is Power. The more you have, the more powerful you can be.

And there is another reason besides the pursuit of knowledge to journey to your inner warrior and other inner parts. Once you experience this warrior energy in journeytime, you are more able to Be that energy in everyday reality in a good way, in balance and harmony and with this part as an ally to your dream for your life and that of your community.

If you are journeying to your inner judge, it may be to find the wisdom to make decisions; to your homeless person in order to learn to let go of things; to your wild one to find spontaneity, passion and joy; to your lover to open and fire up your heart and sexual nature. You can use these journeys to find answers to many questions in your everyday life, and to access wisdom, power and energy to co-create your life.

Defining Your Boundaries

Boundaries are very touchy issues because they are highly personal and there are very few rules governing them that do not include the personal. Each of us creates our own boundaries. When someone reaches the edge of one, our hairs can stand up and our defenses can automatically engage while we REact to past situations when the boundaries were created. Remember that these boundaries are of our own creation and served a purpose at that time – for our survival, safety and ego identity. They are also fluid and at any moment can be reshaped. The problem arises when they get stuck and no longer serve a purpose. Indeed, non-fluid, stuck, rigid boundaries are harmful, preventing us from transforming our lives according to our intentions and the dreams that we hold for ourselves.

A great friend of Eve's, Chad Doberstein, always says 'It helps if you reframe your idea of boundaries as a gate rather than a fence. Understanding and honoring your own and others' boundaries at any given moment allows access to this gate in that by truly seeing the essence of other's inner self, you will find a clear path to the heart. When you come up against your own or others' boundaries, know that this is an opportunity - that with knowledge of this boundary you can acknowledge it, and that you are then able to both enter a powerful place of communion and healing.' In other words, the more we know someone, the more we know the path to their heart and can connect more authentically with them in a way that is comfortable for them in the moment. If our intent remains pure and one of communing and connecting in an authentic way with other, rather than an intent of manipulating other to fulfill one of our own desires or fantasies, we are open to finding the path to both their heart and to our own. This is authentic and ecstatic connection. Chad also states that 'You cannot truly believe someone's yes until you have heard their no'. In other words, until you know that you can trust that the other person will communicate authentically what they are feeling in any given moment, you cannot truly trust that you are on the path from your heart to their heart.

But this is about how we relate to other's boundaries. What about when our own become a prison, become barriers to living our dream. What do we do when we find ourselves stuck within rigid, unchanging boundaries? What do we do when we find ourselves reactively triggered by events over and over again? When we RE-act in unproductive ways? What do we do when we cannot even imagine any other way of being in the world?

Understanding our boundaries will show us the way to open up to new possibilities, to new ways of being. By exploring the edges of the boxes in which we live our lives, our hope is that we will find a way to continuously reassess and recreate these edges moment by moment with consciousness, honesty and compassion. In that way, we can explore the universe outside the box of our own creation, experiencing greater expansiveness of being.

For an example, you are waiting in line and someone cuts in front of you. You feel your hackles rising. You feel you are overly violated. Boundary issue? Your husband, wife, friend, partner, child, parent, arranges to meet you for dinner and cancels at the last minute. You feel infuriated. Boundary issue? A co-worker had lunch on your desk while you were away because his/her desk is messy and the company lunchroom is being painted. A one-time occurrence, but you are so angry you find it hard to speak to them. A boundary issue? You're at the checkout line in the supermarket and the person in front of you spends two minutes digging out the exact change making everyone wait. Boundary issue? A hug from a friend feels a bit too long and too tight. You make an appointment but your friend or co-worker does not show up and forgets to communicate. Boundary issues? For some of you, reading these brings back memories of emotionally sticky edges. For others, some of them sound like familiar boundaries. For a few of you, none bring forth an emotive response.

How about sleeping alone in the jungle, taking a walk on a dark city street, climbing a mountain or communicating with the dead? Our everyday world is defined by our boundaries, for we will generally only allow ourselves to experience whatever is within the walls of the box we have created for ourselves.

If we were to ask you to write down the boundaries defining your everyday life, you might have a hard time. But if we were to ask you to remember the last time your stomach tightened or you couldn't fall asleep because your mind was too active, or to recall an anger or exciting desire that seethed within you causing a loss of appetite – all due to someone crossing one of your boundaries – you might have an easier time remembering. We may not be able to define all of our boundaries but as soon as one is crossed we sure know it. Note that when our boundaries are approached or breached this does not always elicit anger. In some cases it might be exciting to us and fill us with anticipation. We might consciously begin to wonder whether we wish to explore outside of this boundary, as happens when we come close to certain people. It almost always, however, starts our heart racing and engenders some aspect of fear.

Why is this important? Mind, body and spirit. The three are so intertwined that separating them is impossible. You have five minutes before you have to be at work and stop at the coffee stand in the lobby. But today, the person in front of you is talking to the attendant and the conversation goes on and on and on. By the time you get to your desk, you are four minutes late. The person in the lobby doing the talking crossed your boundaries. It was very inconsiderate; the person should have known you were late. The attendant crossed your boundaries – very unprofessional, a polite word would have ended the conversation. Of course, the bus or subway could have been a few minutes late or the cars that caused the gridlock making the commute a little longer; these were also responsible. You may feel that arriving late crossed your own personal boundaries. You don't like being late and are annoyed at yourself for not leaving the house earlier. Whatever the reason, that nervous pain in your side starts to bother you as you sit down at your desk, and it takes several minutes for your rapid pulse to subside, for you to calm your mind and body enough to really start doing your work effectively. Is the above scenario familiar? Could one seemingly minor event affect your entire day, affect your thoughts, your spiritual energy and your health at the same time?

If anything you have read in this section resonated, even a little bit, you might wish to try the following journey.

JOURNEY: Your intention is to ask spirit to show you a boundary that creates the most difficulty for you in your daily life, or that is holding you back from opening up to a possibility you are or are not currently aware of.

Begin as you choose. Ask to be shown the boundary that most often creates problems for you. In this journey, we are asking that you set aside any preconceived thoughts as to how that boundary may appear – trust that what you need most will be unveiled, relax into the journey and get a sense of it. Try not to censor the way that the boundary comes to you, just 'be' with it for a time. From within the journey, allow yourself to ISIS the boundary in its entirety and the effect that this boundary has upon you. Feel the energy associated with that boundary, both that of the boundary itself and of how you feel when it is broached. Feel also the world on the other side of this boundary, outside of the box that you have built for yourself. This is important and may bring information and emotional energy. You may ISIS a scene from your life, whether an actual memory or a representative scene, or you may ISIS a symbolic scene. The boundary may come to you as an entity, and then of course you may dialog directly with it if it feels right.

In any way that feels comfortable to you, you may ask the following questions to your guide(s), spirit, or to the boundary itself.

Q: What is the nature of my upset, excitement or other response and where, within my body, does this exist?

Q: When did I build you? What situation originally caused me to create this boundary?

Q: What purpose did it originally have?

Q: What am I REacting to?

Q: Does this boundary hold any purpose for me in my life now? If yes, ask:

Q: Under what conditions is this boundary helpful, and:

Q: How will I recognize the occasions when this boundary is in my best interests? If no, then:

Q: Why have I held onto it?

Q: What makes this boundary (or you, if you are speaking directly to the boundary) problematic in my life now?

Q: What would my life look like if I didn't RE-act to the boundary in the way that I have done in the past?

Q: What must I do to bring this consciousness into my everyday reality?

Q: What can I do next time this comes up to avoid upset?

Q: What would it look like if I step outside of this boundary?

Q: How can I support this new expanded boundary?

Q: How can I support consciousness of the fluidity in all my boundaries moment to moment?

Q: If I am to let go of this boundary, how can I accomplish this?

If you are letting go of a boundary, it is a good idea to begin in journeytime. You may receive an answer as to how to let go, and a suggestion is to ISIS your boundary being placed in a river. As the boundary floats on the water, notice the way its defined edges become blurry and diffused as it drifts on the current. Ask what actions can be taken in everyday life or journeytime to dissolve the boundary and create fluidity.

Sometimes the answer we get is that we would benefit from more defined boundaries, rather than diffused or expanded ones. In this case you might ISIS yourself in journeytime building walls, or even gates that can expand and contract as needed. Then ask how to be more conscious of boundaries so that we can act 'in the moment', rather than RE-act, and create fluid boundaries that respond to our soul and spirit in ways that are in the higher good of all.

After you have thought about the information you received from this journey and if action is needed, decide what you must do in everyday reality the next time that this same boundary is approached or crossed, when this button is pushed. When you become aware of the energy that you felt in the beginning of the journey, the energy of the boundary being crossed, you become conscious of the boundary in the moment and before you have a chance to RE-act, can consciously recall what you learned from the journey and the information about what actions you need to take. With practice you hold the possibility of making a different choice. Of creating a different - more expanded or more clear firm -boundary. You can take action at the time of this same occurrence, not from the standpoint of your past, but from the present. And, of course, this is fluid. Next Monday, if that same person is in front of you ordering coffee and having that same conversation, you may find yourself acting quite differently.

As always, repeat this journey as often as necessary.

JOURNEY: Your intention is to journey to the gate of a boundary in order to clear the path and connect deeper within any relationship.

This journey can be performed for relationships with loved

ones, but can also be done for relationships with anyone with whom you feel you are bumping against or unclear of their boundaries, and/or they are bumping against yours.

In this example we will use the instance where you feel that when you ask for something within the relationship, you are uncomfortable with hearing 'No'. Be clear that your intent comes from a place of compassion and of wanting authentic connection - to truly hear and be heard, to see and be seen - and be open to not knowing what that will look like.

Begin as you choose. Ask the help of your guides or of spirit in general. ISIS what is revealed to you. Perhaps you will ISIS the person, perhaps the boundary, perhaps the relationship. Gather information and energy. Ask to be shown the boundary. Ask to be taken to the boundary's gate. ISIS the gate as you ask the question and hear the 'No'. Note the gate and the path beyond. Is it clear? Clear the gate in journeytime any way you can. Ask what is blocking the way. Take in the energy of an honorable and clear path to connect heart to heart with the person who said the 'No'. Of course, it may be the path to your heart that needs the most clearing. Continue until the paths are clear and the gate is functional. ISIS the gate in journeytime opening and closing. Give thanks to this boundary, to this gate, for this opportunity to connect and to begin a new way of being.

Now that you have the information, power and energy that spirit has revealed to you, and know the boundary well, honor this gate. Hear the No's for what they are – a gift telling you more about this person. This is an opening, a path, to knowing this person more and more, to connecting with their heart. Through this knowing and through truly hearing and honoring their choices, their experiences, and their being, you will be able to connect to their essence, heart to heart, as boundaries shift moment by moment.

The more you journey to boundaries to which you are RE acting, the more you can be consciously aware of how your boundaries are affecting your life, and of how you can shape and reshape them. Our hope is that this will give you the tools you need to affect change and to become a co-creator of your life and dreams.

Note that even though this journey used a specific scenario in everyday life, in journeytime we described more open-ended requests of spirit. As you journey more and more, you will intuitively know when you wish to be open ended, and when you wish to be specific. In many instances you will gather more energy, wisdom and power by letting spirit show you what is important for you rather than stating what you want to deal with. Play with both approaches. For an example, if you feel stymied at any time in an open ended journey, you can try a more directed approach with specific questions. If you feel you are not getting anywhere useful in a more directive journey, move to a more open approach. Either way, by switching approaches you may find a more meaningful path for proceeding. Trust that, whether in journeytime or everyday reality, you will know the possible ways that you may proceed no matter what occurs, and if you feel lost ask for help from your guides.

This is the beauty of the shamanic journey: asking spirit to be with you at all moments – for maintaining consciousness of and assistance with the cocreation that we call life.

Finding Your Resistance

By now you may have come to the realization that using the shamanic journey to help make changes and to create the life of your dreams is not always an easy path. As said in the introduction, a shamanic journey will make possible a clear unbiased view of yourself, your spirit, your soul and your life. The knowledge, power and energy that you bring back will give you the tools that you need to change those aspects of yourself that you wish to change. But spirit won't make the changes for you. Spirit and the journey will not force you to initiate and carry out the actions necessary to transform your life. That's your job! Remember, the journey is just the beginning. A shaman (or shamanic practitioner) travels to non-ordinary reality in order to gather wisdom, energy and power to affect change in everyday reality. Without that piece, affecting change here, it is just a meditative experience, not a shamanic journey.

You know what they say – if you want change, you have to change.

Sounds easy?

Or is it?

If you have ever felt frustrated that the change which you desire has not manifested as easily and as rapidly as you wanted, read on.

You have the desire to change, you are beginning to understand why you want to change, and you know what to do in order begin the process. Your journey gifted you with the energy, knowledge and power to change – then what's the problem? And there is a problem, isn't there? Why doesn't the change occur at a faster and smoother pace? Or why doesn't it occur at all? The answer is – the resistance is in you!

In order to move in the direction of a new you, you have to get the vision of the old you out of your head. If you react to situations by deferring to the same old actions and patterns that you have always relied upon, then you are not living in the present. You are not living with full consciousness. You propel yesterday into your future, and you find that tomorrow is just a mirror of yesterday. You find that you are always living from your past.

What has to happen for you to move out of your past? Stay connected, get out of your own way, discard old patterns, and live fully and consciously in the present. In this way, in each moment, your actions and choices will flow from your dream for your life, and you will find yourself truly Being present.

So, just how do you get out of your own way?

We often find that the most effective journeys are those with simple and clear intent. In most cases, what you ask for in the journey is what you will receive. (Although remember that at times when you are not getting what you have asked for in the journey, don't stop – spirit may have other ideas for you and those ideas are more important than your ideas.) The following journey is simple and direct and may be used with any issue that you find you want to address.

JOURNEY: Your intention is to learn why you are stuck, why you are sabotaging yourself on a conscious or unconscious level from beginning or completing the change you wish to accomplish in this world.

Begin as you choose and ask:

- Q: Why am I hesitating in carrying out the actions in my life that I know I need to do in order to affect change (or to overcome an issue).
- Q: What is the nature of my resistance and what three steps must I take to overcome it?
- Q: Are there any specific events from my past that I need to resolve or be aware of that are strengthening that resistance? If no, wonderful. But if yes, we suggest you ask:

Q: What is the source of my attachment to my old way of being?
Q: What are the events that created this pattern and what must I do to resolve them so I can remove the resistance? (This may be an issue in itself and require one or more journeys before you continue.)
Q: I have tried to overcome (state the issue) but have not been able to do it. What am I not seeing? What am I missing that is preventing me from succeeding?
Q: What part of me is not allowing me to see what I must see? OR
Q: What part of me is denying that the change is necessary?
Q: How am I benefiting from keeping things as they are? OR
Q: What is fueling my self-sabotage?

If you ISIS the part of you that is preventing you from solving the issue, you can ask your guide or spirit how you can support that part so that you can work together to affect the change that you envision. Or, as you did in the personality part section, you can journey to that part itself and begin to heal it, thus allowing your changes to occur in this reality more smoothly. You can also change the intent of the journey by asking that the Resistance take a physical form and dialogue directly with it. Remember, there are many ways to tackle an issue. Where we give you one suggestion, your imagination – and spirit – can give you hundreds!

Reconnecting or Releasing

Most of the journeys in this book are direct. You have an issue in mind and utilize the shamanic journey to help resolve it. But what happens if your perception of the issue is fuzzy? What if you are not sure if spirit is directing you, not sure of the message, not sure whether to forge ahead or take the leap and let go.

Suppose you have become unhappy with your job. You used to enjoy going to work and now you find that you have lost all enthusiasm about the job, and yet nothing has changed significantly within the work environment that would account for this. But what if your issue is not disconnection from your job and workplace, but rather an ending of this part of your life? What if this disconnection that you are feeling is simply spirit communicating with you that it is time for releasing, for letting go, and for finding a new job? These journeys will help you find clarity so that you can hone your intent regarding any issue, and will help you to listen to your higher self so that you know when it is time to reconnect and when it is time to release.

Reconnecting

We will use the example of apathy, and in this context we will describe apathy as a feeling of being disconnected with a resulting lack of caring, feeling or emotion. We will define apathy as a lack of enthusiasm, passion, interest or concern.

In its broader sense, we are all apathetic about something. If we all truly cared about global warming, we wouldn't be facing an environmental crisis. Even today, many people refuse to admit that global warming is a reality, or they may acknowledge it but have little or no interest in helping to solve the problem. If people are apathetic about the state of animals, they will not care if a state licenses people to kill deer or bears or any other animal that the state feels are over populated, and will be okay with buying chicken and eggs from large agribusiness farms where animals lead abominable lives, and deaths. Or it may be something more mundane that you are apathetic about, that you find it hard to get passionate about. An example of this might be neighborhood community laws. Some people are adamant about having conformity in the exterior of houses within their community neighborhood, and expend a great deal of energy setting up and enforcing these rules such as the same color curtains in all windows facing the front, uniform paint on the exterior, rules about lawns and driveways, while others in the neighborhood fight the rules tooth and nail. Still others are completely apathetic about the issue. They simply can't get up the energy to care about the issue. We think it is safe to say that we are all apathetic about something at some time in our lives.

But what if you find you have an apathetic disconnection with some part of your life, and this apathy interferes with your passion for life itself? What if this apathy grows to encompass integral activities and relationships –spouses or children, jobs and hobbies, activities that you used to love? What if it interferes with your life force, with the spark that makes each of us unique? (Note: This may be different from the clinical definition of depression because the apathy or disconnection may be confined to only certain aspects of life.) How can journeying help in these circumstances?

Note that, as you have found out from the other journeys presented in this text, this journey is only a beginning. Based on what you experience in journeytime, you may find the need to repeat journeys you have done for other issues in order to get sufficient information to begin to change this aspect of your life.

JOURNEY: Your intent is to explore the feeling of apathy or disconnection towards (you supply the rest of the sentence).

Begin as you choose.

From within your journey, we suggest you ask your guide or

spirit:

Q: How have I disconnected from (whatever part of your life you feel disconnected from). Our examples might be:
- the people with whom I have personal relationships?
- the people in my job or community?
- my job itself or other organizations I belong to?
- the activity I used to enjoy?

Q: Why have I disconnected from...?

Q: Is reconnecting in my best interest? If no, consider the questions below in 'Releasing'. If yes, continue.

Q: In what way am I unconsciously supporting this disconnection?

Q: What part of me needs to be supported in order for me to reconnect to...?

After getting the answer to this, you might consider doing a separate journey calling in that part of you in order to find out what you must do to reconnect to and support that part. Rekindle that connection in journeytime first. Then ask, what can you do in everyday life to reconnect?

Releasing

The other side of this coin – disconnecting or releasing – is more difficult. That is because, although it is our belief that there is no true good or bad within nature, only a state of 'what is', in the moment of this impending loss we all find it hard to remember the bigger picture. For an example, all things in nature go through periods of growth and change. The seasons come and go, with times of growth, and times of decay, in a cyclical fashion. Since life began on our planet, many species came into being and passed into extinction long before our species appeared. Their appearance and disappearance was neither good nor bad – it just was. What if your disconnection is not a result of a dis-ease within you? What if the disconnection is just there because it is time to let go of something that no longer serves your higher good, and part of you resists releasing it? The 'it' can be practically anything. Letting go, for some things, may be much more difficult than holding on and trying to reconnect. It is because of this inherent difficulty in letting go that we suggest more questions in this releasing scenario.

If after asking, 'Is this reconnection in my best interest?' you ISIS a No, we suggest you ask the following:

Q: Why is it not in my best interest?
Q: How would this disconnection support me?
Q: What is the message?
Q: Show me what my life would look like without this connection?
Q: How is retaining this connection holding me back or preventing me from growing or changing into the person I wish to be?
Q: What part of me is resisting letting go of this connection? (As above, when you find the part that is resisting, you can journey and dialog directly with it.)
Q: How can I support this part? (If you decide to journey to the part, ask this question directly to it.)
Q: What am I not seeing that keeps me from disconnecting?
Q: Show me the consequences of disconnecting completely.
Q: If it is in my higher good to disconnect, what do I lose? What do I sacrifice?
Q: What do I gain?
Q: How can I disconnect from it gracefully, with the least amount of pain, suffering, inconvenience etc.?
Q: How can I disconnect without burning my bridges behind me? (Note: You may get the answer that bridges need to be burned.)
Q: How can I disconnect while staying balanced and in

harmony with my higher self and with all of creation?

As always, it may be impossible to retrieve answers for most of these questions in one journey. And, as always, we trust that after reading all the questions, you will intuitively know which questions you want to ask first, and that as you hear the answers you will know what to ask next, and add your own questions.

Journey to Past Lives

Many indigenous peoples around the world believe in reincarnation in a very real way. There is no true death for them, just a shapeshift into another form. We will describe two of these traditions.

For the Shuar of the upper Amazon of Ecuador, traditionally, the human form is not thought to be an easy path. Because of this belief in this fierce warrior culture, death was not feared. Once reincarnated, it was thought that a person could go onto another human life, or to a very different way of being. Eve has heard it spoken by the Shuar that the most desired shapeshift after a human dies is to be the rain, or a rainbow. Even if a child died, although they would grieve their own loss, they were happy for the child who, at the moment of death, was able to shapeshift into a new and perhaps easier form. When a person died in traditional Shuar culture, their name was not spoken again. These warriors would much rather die an honorable death in battle than live a life without passion, without what they term 'Arutam' or spiritual life force.

The Shuar were headhunters (shrinking the heads of their enemies) and the stories of this tribe have long been told – and feared. And yet from their point of view of eternal beingness, the shrinking of heads held an important purpose. The heads that a warrior took in battle would be shrunk to avoid the life force spirit of that being, now shapeshifting, to violently avenge their death as well as the loss of their family and community. The headshrinking (or tsantsa) ritual was performed with great honor, in order to put to rest the spirit of the dead. This was thought to be very important not only to prevent retaliation and revenge, but also so that the soul could move on in a good way and leave the anger and pain of this life and death behind.

The Ipishuna and other tribes of the Brazilian Amazon believe that after death the soul seeks refuge inside huge old rainforest trees, residing there while awaiting rebirth. Within the tree they are able to rest until the time comes for them to be reborn. Offerings are made to the souls of the ancestors wherever large trees are found within virgin rainforest.

In our modern disconnected culture, we have lost the rituals and ways to communicate with the dead and to find the wisdom from our ancestors as well as from our own previous incarnations.

JOURNEY: Your intention is to access energy, power and wisdom from your soul essence in its previous life experiences in order to help you understand or deal with an issue that is in your current life.

Begin as you choose. ISIS a shiny, clean, tunnel with two open ends. The beginning of this tunnel is the present, the tunnel proceeds in the direction - past, and the other end comes out into a past life. Ask your guide, or spirit in general, to take you to a life experience that will help you in your current life. ISIS yourself entering this tunnel, walking through it as it becomes darker and darker. Halfway through it is pitch black and, as you continue, it begins to lighten until you see an exit at the other end. Step out into a previous lifetime. Look around you. Is it day or night? Are you outside or inside? Are you alone or with someone? What are you wearing? Look at your feet. Look at your hands. Are you male or female? Young or old? Are you carrying anything? What is the terrain? Are their plants, rocks, mountains, water, animals, birds, etc?

Note that at times you will journey through the eyes of your previous self; whereas in other past life journeys you may see yourself as if watching a movie.

Explore and begin to ask questions. Feel the energy within you deeply, and begin to find the core essence of your soul. You will note the part of you that is different from the you in your current everyday reality. It is a different personality, a different energy. And yet, you will also find a part of you that is unchanging, eternal – your essence, your soul. Ask your guide(s) to accompany you on this journey and to help answer your questions, or alternatively ask the people, plants, animals or other objects you ISIS – the spirits that you come across in the journey that unfolds, including the you in this other life.

Two questions we suggest you ask are:

Q: Why this life? Why am I being led to this life NOW?
Q: Why am I being shown this particular scene in that life?

Begin to take in the information, the energy and the power that is present in THAT previous life and gather what is needed by you now in THIS current life. The memories that you ISIS may be able to open doors for the current you. When you have that information, you may wish to ask be taken to the next important scene in that life. Or, you may wish to experience your death and what happens after. Experience the spiritual realm in between lives. Explore and find out what the soul and spirit realms are like. Spend time in the Bardo state (that time after death that is described in Buddhist texts). Spend time wherever you are led in this journey. Be with your guides and elders. Ask for help and information. Perhaps ask to be taken to yet another life. Be open to where you are taken, even if you find you are not on this planet. Maybe even not as a human. Be open to whatever spirit feels you need to experience right now. You may have a chance to see and be with the souls of important relationships in your life now, whether family, lovers, friends or 'enemies'. Notice the connections.

We suggest that you look deeply into the eyes of beings that appear. Notice and/or ask yourself or the being or your guide:

Q: Do you recognize any that are in your life now?

Q: Are there groupings? What is the eternal purpose of the connection(s)? What is the purpose of the connection in this current life?

Q: Are there patterns of connection from life to life?

Q: What agreements did you make before you were born with this person?

Q: How long have you been together? How many lives?

Q: Is your purpose going well?

Q: Have you fulfilled your agreement?

Q: What karma do you have unfulfilled?

Q: What insights do you gain from meeting these people or other beings in this eternal space?

Q: What do you ISIS of their eternal essence, of their energy?

Q: How is your experience of their eternal essence different from your experience of them in this life?

Q: How do you feel regarding your actions in the past life you have just been shown in this current life?

Q: How do your guides and wise elders feel about your actions and performance while incarnate?

Note that words in English are often inadequate for these questions. We have used words from some cultures that embrace the philosophy of reincarnation, but use the questions that are in your heart. Listen with your heart. The questions and answers may well come nonverbally in journeytime, but words are what we are limited to in writing this book and in describing the journeys.

Of course, this may also take more than one journey. There are many journeys that can be done and repeated again and again to a place of higher perspective. After each journey, you will return with knowledge and energy that you need in this life. This journey comes more from our Western culture's concept of past lives than from current indigenous cultures; however, it is a very powerful tool for soul growth, insight and wisdom.

Journey to Your Essence, The Junction of Soul and Spirit

Eve has studied with Zulu elder, holy man, prophet, healer, artist and storyteller, Credo Vusamazulu Mutwa, for many years. Zulu cosmology describes a complex set of spiritual entities within each individual, during and after life. To simplify, we will describe the two major entities, and for descriptive purposes we will call them the soul and the spirit.

The Buya is the eternal soul. This soul is the entity that is involved in reincarnation, going from life to life, body to body.

The Yena is the Earth-based entity that develops during a single incarnation. We might call it a spirit. This entity maintains the personality and appearance in its light body after death.

The Buya, due to its eternal nature, is far seeing, looking at everything with an eternally broad perspective. This lofty view can be calming and wise. However, if you are unbalanced in that you are living mostly from your Buya, there is no hurry to get anything done. After all, you have eternity.

Alternatively, your Yena has but one lifetime in the physical realm. As such, it is much more attached to material things and to outcome. If you are unbalanced by living more through your Yena, you typically exhibit greed and impatience.

You, as an individual living this life, are the marriage of these two entities. Like any marriage there must be balance of power and communication, compassion and love. Living in balance gives us creative drive and ambition through our Yena spirit, as well as the wisdom of ages and long-term perspective through our Buya soul.

You could say we exist as individuals on the point at which two lineages intersect. One is our blood lineage of Yena: mother matter passing in a long line physically through DNA, as sperm meets egg, creating a new body from the ones who walked before, going far behind us and far ahead of us in time. The Yena who walked before us are our ancestors and, according to Zulu wisdom, these Yena have a vested interest in us, and us in them. They are to be remembered, honored and fed. In this way we enliven them and give them energy to be available to us for assistance in our lives, and in the lives of our descendants. We live knowing that our own Yena will become an ancestor to our descendants in time. Our Yena, after death, will then exist in light body with all our ancestors in a good place, watching over our children and grandchildren, intimately involved with events occurring on the Earth plane.

The other intersecting line is the lineage of our Buya, of our past lives as well as our future incarnations. This lineage holds the energy, power and wisdom from all the soul connections that these lives have built within and between those lives. This is not our bloodline, and yet it holds much importance to us as we live any particular life. Our soul lineage brings us experience, knowledge, connections and helpers, as well as affinities, likes, dislikes, patterns, lessons and familiarity with certain traditions and ways of being.

Accessing both of these intersecting lineages is critical in facilitating balance in our current life. There may be issues within both lineages, as well as deep sources of loving assistance. Spirit attachments, issues and patterns may promulgate through ancestral as well as through past life lineages. Helper spirits and memories may be accessed from both lines. Remembering that we are the intersection of these two lines helps us to create a good life, living as the balanced marriage of both soul and spirit lines. Living in balance allows conscious access to our lineages and the essential energies, memories and wisdom such that we can embody our connection to Source. Accessing and honoring ancestral and past life lineages also engenders peace of mind through the knowledge that after this Earth-based body's life, our Yena spirit will live on, healthy and free, existing with the other ancestors in peace, providing assistance to our descendants and creating a harmonious planet. We also ensure that our Buya soul will be free to go to its place of healing and learning before moving on to a new life in another ancestral bloodline.

By accessing both lineages, we can also gain insight into the purpose of our lives and into the direction that our soul is taking through many lives. The more insight and re-membrance we accrue, the better we can live within the fabric of time and space in our eternal community of soul and spirit.

Of course, we may come back into the same blood lineage again and again, onwards in time, creating webs of soul/spirit connections. A beautiful fabric comes into being as past life and blood lineages may intersect several times. Soul and spirit connections come together over and over within the same Buya line. Conversely, Buya soul lines may drop into ancestral lines from widely divergent cultures with widely divergent Yena ancestral spirit connections.

After life all the Yena Spirits, out of body but still deeply interested in Earthly corporeal life, must be fed and honored. Lost and forgotten Yena must also be helped to find their way to their family lines amongst the Ancestors. All African traditions are clear on this critical practice. These are our communal spirit elders and when our culture dropped this practice of feeding and honoring the ancestors, energetic clouds of hungry Yena resulted throughout our world, negatively affecting our lives and that of our planet.

As a community, our task of clearing these clouds, of helping these hungry spirits find their way home, creates a cleaner and kinder world for our descendants and for all our relations, human and otherwise. When we personally live each moment as a conscious point in each of these lines – remembering, honoring and feeding those that walked before us in both soul and ancestral lines as was done in the old traditions – we are able to ensure that we do not leave residue behind and around us.

Consciously tending this web of lightbodies helps lost entities to find peace. As we live in this mindful manner, we co-create this web – a collective world comprised of both physical and nonphysical components of harmonious energetic resonance – the music of the ages.

JOURNEY: Your intention is to access your Ancestral Yena Spirit blood lineage.

Begin in your chosen manner. ISIS your life spark, your spirit, as a point of light on a long line, heading far into the future and far into the past. ISIS a long line of spirits who walked before you and have made up the body that you inhabit now. ISIS the people in your blood family that you know and who have crossed into spirit realm. See them behind you with many, many others that you did not meet in this life. They may form into groupings. Ask questions to your guide (s) or to those you ISIS.

- Q: What resources lie within your family lineage that can aid you?
- Q: What patterns of those who went before or those who will come after need to be either repeated or avoided now?
- Q: Is there any unfinished business that you can help complete?
- Q: Who are the healers in your bloodline?
- Q: Who are the wise ones?
- Q: The creative muses?
- Q: Who is available to help?
- Q: What help can they offer?
- Q: How would those in your line like to be remembered and fed?

As the journey progresses and you receive more information, more questions and insights will come to mind. Ask them!

You may repeat this journey many times. While you are

journeying, it may help if you hold or keep nearby something that your immediate ancestors passed on to you, or things that remind you of them, or that you know that they liked. We hear of mediums using cigars, rum and other substances to contact Yena, drawing them near with tempting physical objects. You may know or have heard stories about your own bloodline and what they are drawn to. Perhaps you know that your grandmother loved chocolate, or Debussy, or that your Great uncle was a connoisseur of Scotch malt. Make use of whatever information you have of your ancestors' affinities and of the time that they walked the Earth and have these things available to know them more and more, call them in, to remember them, and to honor them.

JOURNEY: Your intention is to access your Eternal Soul Buya lineage.

If you have not yet done so, this is the time to take the Journey to Past Lives.

Once you hold both these important lineages consciously, you can move on to the next journey.

JOURNEY: Your intention is to bring into consciousness the intersection of your soul and spirit lines – The Eternal Soul Buya lineage and the Ancestral Spirit Yena lineage.

Begin this journey in your chosen manner. ISIS yourself as a point of light at the intersection of two lines. First, ISIS yourself on the ancestral spirit bloodline (as you did before) and reconnect with all your known and unknown ancestors and descendants. Then ISIS yourself on the line of your known and unknown past and future lives, your soul Buya lineage extending into the past and future. Your current life is the intersection of these two lines. Feel the energy, power and wisdom that you gain from each of these lineages, and feel within you your unique soul Buya and spirit Yena essences. Feel the balance between the two. Ask your guide(s), spirit, or feel out for yourself:

Q: Can you ISIS the perspective of your eternal soul Buya, farseeing and patient, tranquil and wise?
Q: Can you ISIS the finite perspective of your spirit Yena, ambitious and driven, filled with creative energy and an acquisitive longing?
Q: How do you act and view the world from the perspective of your Buya? Of your Yena?
Q: Where do you need balance?
Q: Are you living too much from your Buya (with procrastination, inertia, withdrawn from the physical, perhaps too spiritually seeking, disconnected and distracted)? Are you living too much from your spirit Yena (too material seeking, with impatience, attachment, shortsightedness, and selfish ambition)?

When you ISIS an area of imbalance, try viewing it from the perspective of your other half, of your eternal buya or finite yena. Does this bring a broader perspective, some peace of mind and heart? Does this wake you up to the fire of your creative drive, your life force and joy of the physical, the drive to manifest your dreams?

Q: How can you create balance within yourself as the marriage of soul Buya and spirit Yena?
Q: How can you maintain this balance and remain conscious of and take action through both the eternal Buya soul and finite Yena spirit parts of yourself?

Repeat this journey often, especially with the intention of finding balance and solution to any issue, decision or event in your life. In this way you can view any life issue from the perspective of both your eternal ethereal and finite earthly selves.

Spiritual Life Force – Finding Your Arutam

The Shuar speak of the concept of Arutam as a spiritual force that can be sought by an individual to enhance their life force and spirit, and to give meaning to their life. Similar spiritual forces are described by many other cultures; however, we will use the Shuar cosmology to describe this journey.

Again, we will remind you that English is not a very spiritual language and so it is often difficult to translate spiritual concepts from such languages as Shuar, Quechua, Tupi and other indigenous languages into English. Rather than trying to define it intellectually, it is best to learn the concept and familiarize yourself with this spiritual force by direct experience in journeytime.

When a traditional Shuar goes on a vision quest, Eve was told that the spirit of Arutam often presents as a jaguar, an anaconda, a volcano or another force of nature. When you seek Arutam you are on the hero/heroine's journey, and the Shuar are a warrior people. Although you may or may not come across jaguars and other forest beings, in this journey you can expect strengthening challenges and acts of great courage.

When you journey to seek your Arutam, you are asking to meld with this strong spiritual force, giving strength to both your physical and your spiritual life and providing clarity of a combined spiritual and physical direction.

JOURNEY: Your intention is a quest for Arutam and to bring this life force into your being.

Begin as you choose. Ask your guide(s) or spirit to assist, and state your intent. Be open to what presents itself to you, and ask questions. 'Are you my Arutam, and if not can you take me to it?' You may find that you are asked to do something in journeytime which requires great courage. Though this journey is relatively easy to explain, for some it can be a long and difficult one to perform. The anaconda may not just meekly appear so you can ISIS its power. But it may open its mouth and invite you in. If that happens, our advice is to accept. Whatever challenges spirit wishes you to overcome, or actions you are to fulfill, we suggest you do so. Whatever follows from saying yes is likely to be both unexpected and wildly empowering.

Earlier in the text, we spoke at length about feeling the energy from within a journey and making conscious efforts to recall and 'be' that energy when returning to everyday reality. We invite you do that again with whatever situation you are presented with. In the example of being swallowed by the anaconda, feel the energy that the snake spirit is sharing with you. Take a moment to bask in that energy. Breathe it in – shapeshift and become one with it. Now continue with the journey and accomplish what you are asked to do. And if instead your Arutam comes to you as a dove or a raccoon, don't reject them by asking them to take you to the anaconda. Arutam is not defined by our words or wishes. It is defined by spirit – the wisest teacher of all!

Shamanic Mirrors

The shamanic path makes frequent use of the concept of shamanic mirrors.

Anything can be a mirror for you, anyone or any situation, and teach you about who you are. As it says over the door at the Temple at Delphi where the Oracle sat in shamanic trance, 'Above all know thyself'.

What do we mean by a mirror? A mirror is someone or something that mirrors you.

How can you identify a mirror? Anyone to whom you have an emotional response is your mirror. The stronger the emotive response, the more accurate and important the mirror. This is yet another way in every day life that spirit communicates with you.

Mirrors may feel positive or negative, although these labels have little value.

Think of someone who infuriates you in every way. What is it about this person that you hate? This is in you. In general, the reason why we become infuriated is that this is a part of ourselves that we have put a great deal of energy in denying, and in making sure it never comes out and is never seen. By owning this as a part of ourselves, we can let go and free up the energy we have been using so hard in order to suppress it. This will increase our vital energy resulting in a lightness of being, fullness of vitality and increased creativity. Note that releasing this 'negative' self does not mean that you will act in ways counter to your higher good, only that the energy that you formerly used to ensure that this part remained suppressed will be freed up. In journeytime, ask how you can express this part in a good way. (See also 'Finding Your Shadow Self'.)

Now think of the person you admire most in the world, of whom you are in awe. What about that person do you admire or even envy? Make note that envy and jealousy, when viewed as spiritual messages, can be important treasure maps to finding our whole self. Again, by owning that part of ourselves, we can let go and free up the energy we are habitually using to block ourselves from shining fully in the world, from living full out and expressing that awesome way of being.

JOURNEY: Your intention is to access the hidden parts of yourself that are shown to you through your mirrors.

Begin as you wish. ISIS a strong mirror for yourself, one that brings out a strong emotion in you. It could be someone you know, a famous personality, a historical person or even a fictional character. Remember, the stronger your emotional response to this person the more important a mirror he or she is. Feel the emotion. Be 'one' with that emotion for a while. The anger, the awe, the sadness, the envy – feel what you feel. Don't think about what you feel, just feel it – be with it!

Now, ask your guide or spirit:

Q: What is it about this mirror that creates the emotion?

Feel that quality within yourself. Notice how locked up this part of you is. Whether you view the emotion as positive or negative, the part is just as hidden. ISIS that part being constrained in some manner, being caged in, tied up or trapped in a cave. Break it free. Release it.

Ask your guide or spirit:

Q: How will releasing this mirror (the part that is hidden within you) free me up in my life to be fully me. To be in closer harmony with my higher good, with my higher self.

Q: What can I do in everyday life to support that release and sustain that new freedom. Don't forget, at the end of this journey you will have met a new part of yourself. That part will need to be nurtured now that it is out in the open.

> What better way of finding out how to nurture it than journeying to it and asking.

You may find over time that these answers will come quickly to you in everyday life without taking time out to lie down and journey. Become conscious of the fact that whenever you are conscious of a trigger, or when you are feeling of a strong emotional response to someone, you are seeing a shamanic mirror of yourself.

As with many of the journeys and concepts discussed in this text, this journey may or may not be easy depending on the level in which you explore the information, power and energy that you bring back from journeytime into your everyday life. At any level, the act of releasing this energy will defuse and expand the boundaries of the box in which we live. Even though that creates an environment of personal growth within, we often find ourselves stubbornly resisting that kind of change. Do not be surprised by, and perhaps even expect, resistance. Be compassionate with yourself, release the blocks and remember to ask for help from spirit.

Understanding Our Teachers

When we think of teachers, we think of individuals working in educational settings: schools, universities, workshops given by authors and other experts in their field, etc. But these are only a very small portion of the teachers we connect with through our lives, and not even the most important ones. Our true teachers are all around us, if we care to look. They are the people with whom we come into contact in our everyday lives – the bus or taxi driver, the store clerk, the stranger on the subway, or the person who stands next to us in line while we wait to buy our coffee. The people in our offices, the woman who sits at the desk near us, and the person who delivers our mail are all our teachers. Indeed, practically everyone we come in contact with, whether we know them or not, hold lessons for us. Our teachers are the people who bring us joy as well as those who annoy us, who cause us stress and who make life more difficult for us (see also the section 'Shamanic Mirrors').

The people in many of the journeys described in this text – the person in the supermarket searching for change, the attendant who didn't cut short the conversation while you had to wait, even the person who was doing the talking – all of these people are our teachers. They each hold something sent for us to learn.

Our teachers are not always people either; they can be non-human beings. Animals, plants, wind, rain, oceans, mountains or even those without physical form such as tastes, smells, nighttime dreams and many other entities and events may be important teachers.

We do not want to get into the argument of free will versus predestination in this book. We do not wish to argue the concept of synchronicity, that there are no coincidences in life. We will not suggest that in order to learn a lesson about patience, spirit placed that person in front of you who searched for the correct change and made you wait in line. We will suggest that in each of these cases spirit offers you an opportunity to learn something, that is if you care to listen to the messages and accept the teaching.

Learning is not always an easy thing for us to do. This is, in part, because accepting the opportunity to learn would also mean accepting the idea that our teachers do not always present lessons to us in the way we would like them to. It would mean understanding that the people who push our buttons, who cross our boundaries and who annoy us are just as much our teachers as those who we pay to teach us. It means we have the continually present opportunity to grow and learn, to see behind the veil and to live consciously, looking at the world around us and seizing the opportunities to learn more and more about ourselves. By looking at events in this manner, we can receive guidance on being the person we wish to be. Remember, most people walk the shamanic path in order to be 'better people', whatever better means to you in the moment. The definition of 'better' changes the more you commune with spirit. It is a life characterized by continual growth and self-improvement. Conscious awareness of all of our teachers is essential in moving us along the shamanic path we have chosen.

JOURNEY: Your intention in is find out what you can learn from the people who push your buttons.

To be honest, we feel inadequate in suggesting the following questions. We are sure that by this time you will think of people and situations that have gotten out of hand and will instinctively know exactly what questions to ask of spirit. We will list them anyway. Use them as is, or allow them to trigger your thought process into thinking of questions that you need answered. And with even more honesty, our hope is that this will become so natural to you that you will not need to journey in the sense of taking time out of everyday life to ask questions. We hope that you, in every moment, will live in a continual journey with the world around you, asking the questions instantaneously and consciously communing with spirit and with your higher self to co-create the person you wish to be.

Here is a journey for times when you wish to go back to situations which you feel may hold a message for you that wasn't clear in the moment. In journeytime, relive the experience when your 'teacher' presented you with a lesson, allow it to unfold further, and ask for help from your guide(s) or from spirit. Alternatively, in journeytime, you could dialogue directly with the spirit of the teacher. Try to feel the experience along with the energy and emotions associated with it. Hold the experience fresh in your mind and ask your guide(s) or spirit to allow you to ISIS the answers to the following questions, or ask them to the teacher you ISIS:

Q: What triggered my emotional response?

Q: Why do I have that 'button' the teacher pushed in the first place?

Q: When and under what circumstances was this button created in me?

Q: What use does this button hold for me now? What/How does it teach me?

If the answer is that this button is no longer of use, ask:

Q: How can I discard or transmute this trigger?

If the answer is that this button continues to teach you, ask:

Q: What am I not understanding?

Q: How does this trigger support me and how can I accept that support in a positive way?

Q: What must I do in order to begin to learn how I can react differently when a person pushes the button?

Q: What part of me (my personality) was most angered? (You know what this means now that you have another part of you to connect with, don't you?)

Q: What must I do to ACT to those button-pushing incidences from the 'present', not REACT from the past?

Q: How can I become conscious of situations that might result in a button being pushed in order that I can choose to act in a different way?

Q: How can I become aware that a button is being pushed before I overreact?

Q: How can I ensure that I hear the message and learn the lesson?

And now, the hard questions: (Also see 'Shamanic Mirrors'.)

Q: What about the teacher is in me?

Q: How am I similar to the teacher?

Q: What do I admire (or what part of me is supported) by the actions of the teacher that triggered my response? (If you sense a part that needs to be supported, ask your guide, spirit or, of course, journey to the part.)

Q: What do I dislike about the teacher and where is a similar characteristic energy lodged within me?

Q: What part of the energy associated with that trigger do I need to bring into my life? Or:

Q: What energy do I need to accept as within me?

Q: What part of me do I need to stop trying to hide in order to free up energy for other purposes in my life?

Obviously, this may not be a single journey. As a matter of fact, each question could be viewed as a separate journey. But we are confident that instinctively you will know how to break it up into the journeys you need to do at this time in your life.

Energetic Protection

Each of us, whether consciously or unconsciously, absorbs and discharges energy. Have you ever received a letter filling you with joy and excitement because it announced something you wanted very much to happen – a new job offer, that special person in your life coming for a visit, an offer to publish your novel, or any one of a hundred other exciting possibilities? Did you ever find that when you came into someone else's presence, even before you could tell them why you were so excited, they smiled? And the opposite – has that ever happened? You suddenly feel sadness come over you and subsequently a friend or colleague comes over to you and tells you their bad news? In the first case, you were sending out joyfully upbeat energy that was picked up by another. In the second, you picked up and absorbed someone else's sad downbeat energy. Absorbing someone else's energy or having another absorb yours happens unconsciously all the time and that energetic exchange may not always be in the higher good of either person. By taking in what is not yours you may, without meaning to, give up control over part of your body, mind and spirit – the part that dictates your attitude in the moment. On the other hand, picking up others' energy is an important part of divination. Of the diagnosis of problems when doing healings. How can you ensure that these energy exchanges occur consciously and productively, rather than on a subconscious level, and without intent. If you are happy, sad, angry or feeling any other emotion strongly enough, that energy will surround you unconsciously. The same is true for others, and you can learn to control this - to block others' energy from entering you when not wanted, and to allow it when you need to. The key is conscious attention to energy flow. With time and practice, this control can be fine tuned. We will begin simply with protection, and shielding yourself from external energy is what this next journey is all about.

Note that some people are empathics and are extremely sensitive and open to emotional energy; some are intuitives and open to informational energy. As stated previously, we all access spirit, energy and information differently. Consciousness of your own unique method of access is helpful in this practice.

JOURNEY: Your intention is to ask your guide or spirit for a symbol that will prevent outside energy from entering you, to learn how to activate that symbol, and to ask your guide or spirit to bring that symbol into you so that it is present whenever you need protection.

Note: You may wish to have a pencil and paper within easy reach before you start this journey.

By now, you have learned one thing about the journeys in this book: they are filled with questions. We are also confident that by now, you have discovered the easiest way to frame your intention to spirit so that you can get the most out of each journey. Framing questions and intentions is as individual as journeys are, and each person finds their own style. Spirit guides also have individual personalities, and what works for you with one guide may not be the best approach with another.

Eve has one guide that never speaks a word and yet communicates information and transmits power beautifully. But how Eve frames her questions to this guide is very different from the way she questions others. She communicates with that guide telepathically. (We know this sounds funny when in journeytime everything is telepathic, yet what we mean is that she communicates without dialogue.) We suggest you read the entire journey each time, taking in all the suggestions we make, and then framing the intention and questions by tailoring them specifically to your needs in the journey moment. This is, of course, true for all journeys.

From the point in the beginning of your journey when you

state your intention, ask your guide or spirit to show you a symbol that you can use to prevent outside energy from entering you. ISIS whatever spirit shows you. In the event that you experience a geometric shape, it is important that you remember it. Most people will do so simply by asking that they remember, but if you find that you are not one of those people, at this point request that your guide or spirit please wait a moment. Come out of your journey, draw the shape or make note. Then return to the journey state. Your guide will usually be waiting at the exact point you left him/her/it.

Next, ask your guide or spirit how to activate the symbol. Experience what the symbol will do – or what you must do – in order for the symbol to begin working. If the symbol is an egg, walnut or other closed shape, will it surround your energetic field or must you go into it? If it is an animal guide, what will the animal do? If it is a geometric shape, what actions will the shape take to protect you? Be completely open; take in whatever you experience. Ask the symbol you have ISISed that it be semi-permeable, letting in whatever is in your higher good and excluding whatever is not. When your guide shows you how the symbol is activated, feel the energy from the activated symbol coursing through and/or surrounding your body (depending on the nature of the symbol). Take a deep breath, and breathe it in. Experience the energy of your symbol going into your heart, and know that this is part of the love, compassion and understanding spirit has for each of us.

Now, return your attention to your guide or to spirit in general, and ask that the symbol itself come into you, become part of you to reside within you, so that it will always be there when you need it. Imagine the symbol in the space above you. Lift your arms, cup your hands, and draw your hands to your chest over your heart space. Breathe in deeply when your hands touch your body. Feel the energy of the symbol as it enters you. Now repeat that process once more, only this time bring your hands down over the top of your head onto your crown chakra. Again, deeply breathe in the energy of this protection symbol as you bring it into your body with your hands.

In our personal experience, this last part is very helpful. Ask the symbol that is now part of you to activate itself whenever it is needed. ISIS it activating again at this point. Again feel its energy racing to every part of your body. Be with that energy in the full knowledge that you now will be protected from outside energetic sources, whether sent to you by accident or design.

In everyday life, you can call on your protective symbol when you know you are stepping into energetically taxing situations. We know people who put on imaginary bee suits complete with helmets, or surround themselves with huge eggshells or glass boxes for protection. The way the protective symbol comes to you can take any form. Activate your symbol whenever you feel the need for energetic protection, such as when you step in front of an audience or into a crowd of strangers, and whenever you do healings.

It is our belief that spirit speaks to us all, often by sending an extraneous thought into our heads. Most people, most times, ignore that thought. We're suggesting that you listen. The more you listen, the more you will recognize spirit's 'voice' and the more mutual trust will develop. If you never pay any attention, the 'voice' may get weaker or stop altogether.

If you walk into a room, are on a bus, in a classroom, in the office, or somewhere else and for no reason you just think, if only for a second, about the symbol that you received – spirit is speaking to you. Another's energy is searching for a place to invade. You learned how to activate your symbol. We suggest that when this occurs, just do it! Don't intellectualize. Don't stop and wonder who or why. It doesn't matter. Just consciously, in everyday reality, energize the symbol. You don't have to understand why you are doing it, only that you are doing it. Feel the energy rushing from your heart throughout your body. Give voice, only in your head if you can't speak out loud: 'I do not give you (the searching energy) permission to enter me. Seek out the Universal energy. There you will find peace.' Imagine a stream of light coming towards you and then returning upward towards the sky, out into the Universe. This way, the energy may not harm another being, but will return to its original source. For all energy was born in and returns to the Universal flow. Then, continue with whatever you were doing. This whole process can happen within an instant, and only you will be aware of the entire episode!

If possible, get a physical representation of the symbol. It could be a small glass or crystal egg, a real walnut, a small carved figure of the animal, or whatever shape represents the symbol that you were gifted with. If a geometric shape, perhaps you could draw it and have it laminated so you can carry it in your wallet or pocketbook. Or have a jeweler make this symbol to wear around your neck. When the symbol activates itself, or when you decide that you need protection, holding the symbol in your hand is a powerful aid in helping you fully feel the strength of spirit's connection protecting you.

Finding Your Inner Indigenous Self (Restoring Connection and Harmony While Living With Gratitude and Honor)

Most people recognize that Mother Earth is suffering through the actions and choices of our human community and many people believe that we, in the industrialized world, are in the process of destroying her. But there are communities who still exist today, conscious of Mother Earth and Father Sky as their creators. We term these people indigenous, and we have much to learn from them.

Indigenous peoples live each day in harmony with nature, honoring Mother Earth and Father Sky. They understand that we are literally born of these parents: Mother Earth, who gifts us the physical matter that forms every cell in our bodies and Father Sun, who gifts us the energy that sparks life itself. This way of life is characterized by a pervasive consciousness of the ongoing interaction that we have with Mother Earth and Father Sky. With gratitude as the principal motivator for all their actions and choices, native peoples hold the interconnectedness of all life in mind throughout their lives. All decisions, both individually and as communities, are made by taking into account how their choices will affect Earth and Sky. In addition, the characteristic nature of these traditions takes into account how all actions affect others – not only humans, but also all our relations – now and in the future. Indigenous people are conscious of the flow of time and space, of the phases of the moon and of the solar and stellar movements. They are in tune with the plants, animals, soil, waters, winds, mountains, etc., fully connected with the Universe in which they abide and of which they are a part.

This is the shamanic way, living fully present to the spiritual nature of our physical reality and understanding that there is no separation between the physical and the spiritual. When you live in the moment – present and conscious, with honor and gratitude – the result is a harmonious and gentle walk through our lives. The more presence we cultivate, the more conscious we are of our spiritual physicality. With this consciousness comes an awareness of our footprints on Mother Earth, and how our walk affects Earth and Sky and the future generations of all our relations.

When walking in the jungle with the Shuar, Eve could not help but notice the intimate relationship that these fierce warrior people have with the land around them. They have a deep love of the plants and animals that cohabitate their homes and their awareness even extends outward, several days walk from their long houses. Eve says, 'Many times have I walked beside a Shuar who will stop to notice a change in the forest, a plant that looks different from the last time that they walked that path. Then that individual will gather with elders and discuss at length what this change might signal, and how as a community they will change their actions because of this. Their goal is to protect the forest and all life. And if it means walking a different path to allow that single plant to grow undisturbed by human contact, then that is what they will do. Time and time again I cannot help but feel humbled, knowing that I am not sure if I would notice a change in the plants on my own block, let alone an entire forest. Now, through my love of nature, I strive to be more and more conscious of the flow, of my place in this flow and of my place in community.'

So how can we cultivate this presence, this consciousness? How can we learn from this indigenous way of being? Are we indigenous to Mother Earth too? Were we not also born of her?

It is likely that if we are of an industrialized culture we were not brought up connected to the flow of nature in our everyday lives. This disconnection has muddied our intent for our lives, to the detriment of Mother Earth. To paraphrase John Perkins, shaman and author of many books, including *Shapeshifting* and

Confessions of an Economic Hitman, it is not Mother Earth who is in jeopardy – it is us. When the time comes that Mother Earth realizes that we will continue to destroy her rather than create harmony, she can always shake us off her with no more effort than a dog shaking off loose fleas in her hair. Mother Earth will continue for millions of years, with or without us as the dominant species. Just like the little forest plant signals a change to the Shuar, Mother Earth is giving us signs that need to be heard; signals that our actions need to change for the benefit of Father Sky and of her, for the benefit of all our relations, for the benefit of future generations. It is because of the love, understanding and compassion that our Mother Earth has for us that she continues to alert us to the obvious: by our actions we have become disconnected, altering the balance that sustains all life.

She gives us warning signs because she IS our Mother – for we, too, are indigenous to this earth, and it is time we realize this and treat our Mother Earth and Father Sky with honor.

In any of our bloodlines, you only need to go back a few generations to find communities living closer to the Earth, living in the flow, with harmony and honor, connected to spirit and aware of our interconnectedness with Earth, Sky and all our relations. These ancestors were aware that they were setting the stage for us, their descendants. Their decisions were always made by taking into account the effect on Earth and Sky, on all their relations, and on their children and grandchildren for seven generations ahead.

Yet, it is commonly held that those of us brought up in industrial cultures are not indigenous; that those of us who live in communities that have lost the way of connecting and living in harmony with our Mother and Father have no right to the claim of being called indigenous. How can we reconcile this if we are all part of this same Mother Earth? How can those of us who were brought up in an industrialized culture, but want to connect deeper to Mother Earth and Father Sky, find our indigenous core?

How can those of us who wish to live in an Earth honoring way, in gratitude and harmony, and to walk softly on this Earth, claim that we are also children of nature, also indigenous to Earth? And how can we deny that it is truly this claim that can save our Mother from dishonor and destruction, the realization of our indigenous nature?

We can ask our indigenous ancestors who lived close to the Earth. We can learn from our ancestors, and from those current lineages who maintain these indigenous ways. We can find our inner indigenous self to restore that harmony and find our deep connection with Mother Earth and Father Sky.

JOURNEY: Your intention is to connect with your indigenous ancestors to find your indigenous core.

Begin as you choose. Ask to be taken back along your personal bloodline.

Ask your ancestors for help and to be shown the ways in which your ancestral family lived in harmony with nature.

The details of the journey may or may not be important, but feeling the energy of this way of life is. Feel this connection. Breathe it in. Become one with it. Take in the honor, the knowledge of the flow of nature, the deep connection. Feel the gratitude to Mother Earth and Father Sky, to spirit, to all who walked before us.

Ask to be reminded of this way of living in harmony. Thank the ancestors in your bloodline. Thank, also, those native peoples who continue this honoring way of life such that it is available to us even today, who have maintained their connection and honor.

Ask to feel the love of Mother Earth and Father Sky who gave you the gift of life.

Ask how you can bring this indigenous way of living, this energy, into your own life, into your own culture, into your own family and community at this time.

Ask how you can maintain and deepen your connection with

Mother Earth and Father Sky.

Ask how you can find presence, balance and harmony, to stay conscious of the flow and the interconnectedness between nature, yourself and all your relations. Feel your indigenous core and become aware of your indigenous nature.

Ask for an ancestral or other guide to be with you at times when connection seems to be weakened, when your indigenous core needs help manifesting in your life.

And ask what you can bring to our global community from your lineage, what unique medicines you hold to rebuild an Earth honoring world of harmony and balance.

JOURNEY: Your intention is to find your place (or role) in the various communities you belong to in order to begin the process of restoring balance to each.

Please note: We are suggesting that you begin in the most basic of communities you belong to and work outward from there. But after reading our plan for your journey (or journeys), please begin wherever you wish.

From the journey space, ISIS (don't forget – imagine, see, intuit, sense) yourself in your own home surrounded by family and/or close friends. ISIS each person and ask yourself, how does that person support me in life and how do I support them in return? Feel the energy that is associated with each person and with the energetic flow of that connection. If it feels right and you know that there is balance and harmony in your energetic exchange, that you support each other as much as possible, move on to the next person. Note that in this journey you are not looking to judge the quality of the exchange, but more the balance. You are becoming conscious of the interconnected web within which we live on this Earth. If the energetic exchange does not feel balanced, or if you get the feeling that there is a destructive effect on the web of life within this community, dialog with that person in journeytime in order to understand why the exchange is not as it should be. Find out what your role is in the community and what must be done in everyday reality to strengthen it and bring it back into harmony and balance. Then continue visiting the other people in your immediate community.

In your next journey, repeat the journey above in your work community, beginning at your office or a place of work. Call into your journey the people you associate with in your professional life. Ask the same questions as you asked in the first journey.

Continue by journeying to the other communities that you have roles in, and of course it goes without saying that you may take several journeys as you see fit. You may journey to explore the balance and your role and effect on your spiritual communities, the organizations where you volunteer, hobbies such as playing cards or golf, political clubs you belong to, etc. Any activity that you do on a regular basis that allows you to interact with other people can be included in this journey. There may well be some overlap in people involved in your communities as circles fall upon other circles, and you may find that your role in and effect on each community is very different. As the communities become larger, you may journey to individual connections with people, or you may journey to the community itself, asking your role in the community, and asking the community's role in the world. ISIS the community's activity or purpose for existing. For an example, you may journey to the spirit of 'golf' or 'art' and speak directly to it. You may not support 'golf' or 'art' in the same way that you support your best friend, but you can find out how 'golf' or 'art' supports you and how you support it. The same with the community of golfers, and how the community supports the community of Earth, now and in the future. The same holds true for any organization or community that you are journeying to, and that includes communities of nonhuman entities: the waters, the mountainous apus, the trees... A key word to remember in all of these journeys is harmony. Your goal is to see how the people and organizations in all aspects of your life support you and help you to live in balance and harmony within yourself, with those around you and with Mother Earth and Father Sky. And to see how you do the same for others. If you feel that the organization or community is not supporting Mother Earth or is not in harmony with Her, ask what you can do to begin to restore that harmony.

Now explore the larger web. Begin from your home and ISIS yourself floating upwards into the sky. Imagine you are a rocket moving slowly away from the earth. Pause that upward flight when you ISIS your local community: your city or county. Ask of that city or county the same questions you have asked before: How do you support me in my life and how do I support you in your life or existence? Make sure you ask how you can strengthen your connection in order to create harmony with your life and with all our relations. Ask how to support future generations and the Earth realm, and what you can do in everyday reality to be conscious of these energetic supportive connections such that you can make use of them and so that you can give back.

When you have that information, continue upward, stopping again when you ISIS your region or country. Ask the same questions. Make sure you ISIS what support you could give your land that would fulfill your collective intent or dream (always with balance and harmony and keeping in mind the effect on all our relations both current and future generations). Ask what role you could embrace that would support this intent and find out what you can do in everyday reality to embody that support and manifest the intent or dream with honor. When you are satisfied that you have the answers, continue upward in your journey until you ISIS our planet, and then our galaxy and universe. ISIS Mother Earth circling within the black void of space. Ask her the same questions. ISIS what you can do in everyday reality, not only to support her, but to have Mother Earth increase her support of you and of our collective dream of continued life. Ask how to deepen the connections. Communicate with the celestial energies, with the atmosphere, with the star that we call the Sun, and with all the stars in the Sky. Communicate your wishes for deeper connection, mutual support, harmony.

These series of journeys are designed for the following purposes:

To give you a complete picture of yourself in the world, and of how you live in community.

To find areas where there are blocks or imbalances in your relatedness, and to deepen your connection with your inner Self.

To understand your role within the communities you belong to.

To help you in walking consciously with honor, supporting your intent for your life, and your collective intent for the world we live in.

After experiencing the first journey in this section, the intent is also to bring into your conscious life indigenous ways of living conscious of the web of interconnectedness, and of your place in this ever changing, flowing web.

Each journey will give you information as to how you can come into more balance and harmony with the people in your life, as well as with the world around you. You may be given a new energetic feel, a new way of walking in life, a new role, or new actions to take. The actions you ISIS may, at times, seem trivial. Don't minimize them by thinking they are insignificant. Change can occur in our communities with actions as simple as telling your wife or husband that you love him or her more often, not tossing a used paper cup out the window of your car, or not buying bottled water that comes from half way around the world and using filtered tap water instead. You may be given actions that are unexpected; trust them and try them out. Our experience is that you will often be surprised by spirit's answers and by the truth in the information obtained through journeys. Spirit will guide you, and this guidance will change over time as you are readied to hear more - and to take more action.

Our hope is that by becoming conscious of our role in this interconnected world, and by finding our indigenous self, we can shapeshift the world. In the words of our indigenous brother Ipupiara Makunaiman from the Brazilian Amazon, all change comes from within. By shapeshifting yourself, by shifting your energy and focus, by being more in harmony with your higher purpose, by being conscious of the interconnected web and of nature, by finding your role in your community(s) and by living in conscious harmony with our Mother Earth – together, we can, we will – we must - shapeshift our world.

Journey to the Stars

Many brave experiencers willing to share their stories report encounters with beings from other star systems. Eve has worked extensively with experiencers Ipupiara Makunaiman whose tribe claims to descend from the Plaeides, and Vusamazulu Credo Mutwa, author of *Zulu Shaman* and *Indaba My Children*, whose tribe claims to descend from Sirius, as well as the late researcher John Mack MD, author of *Passport to the Cosmos* and *Abduction*. Most indigenous cultures take for granted the relationship between Earth dwellers and those from other planets. Encounters have been reported that are felt by the experiencer to be very helpful. However, some encounters seem to be more helpful to the being from the stars than to the Earthling. Information and intent may be difficult to understand due to the extreme variance in life purpose and experience, as well as the capacity for emotion and cognitive thought. Language can also be difficult as, in our language, there may not be words to describe the concepts and things from the point of view of star beings. Ask your own guides for help, and keep your intent clear, ready to end the journey if it becomes difficult to understand or uncomfortable in any way.

Whether you are an experiencer yourself, or whether you hold this possibility true or not, there is much power, energy and wisdom available from the celestial realm.

JOURNEY: Your intention is to journey to the stars in a safe way to obtain wisdom, energy and power. In your intent, if you wish to be more specific, you may add that you want wisdom, energy and power that will help you deal with a particular issue in your life at this time.

Begin as you choose. ISIS a dark void. ISIS the universe and all the constellations coming into view as you fly through space.

Ask your guide(s) to be with you, and ask to be taken to wherever is most helpful for you today.

Become aware of what is all around you, and whether you journey to a specific place or just to deep space - explore. Ask questions of whoever or whatever comes to you, including the stars, planets and other entities whether physical or not.

If you have a sense that you have been to a place before, ask if it was in this life or another. Ask to be reminded of any information that you received in that previous visit. Ask what lessons you were taught and whether you completed the lesson(s). If not, ask what you can do this time in order to better take in the wisdom or energy or power from the star beings that is aligned with your dream for your life. Ask for an interpreter if you find the concepts hard to understand. A being who can make the information cogent for you as an Earthling.

You may find helpful allies and guides through these star journeys. Ask if you can return for guidance, energy and power whenever you find the need. Ask how they would like to be contacted and what assistance they are there to give. Thank them and ask what they would like of you.

Shifting Dis-ease to Ease

Earlier, in Dealing with Dis-ease, we suggested that you journey to a dis-ease, and after dialoging with it, change its appearance. The hope is that by changing the nature of the dis-ease in alternate reality, you will also change the nature of the dis-ease in everyday reality. The following journeys deal with dis-ease on a deeper level. By accepting the challenges that we face as spiritually relevant, our hope is that we can live in a state of grace.

You may have heard the saying, 'We are spiritual beings having a physical experience.' In this physical realm that we call Earth life, we live in a body with sensations, emotions and thoughts. Our time on Earth is filled with many challenges and limitations. As we grow and experience life, we begin to notice that other beings have different bodies, different families, different lives, different experiences and different challenges.

Sometimes our thoughts are that we love our experiences. Sometimes we become frustrated with our limitations and challenges. Sometimes we wish we had other bodies and other lives. Sometimes we feel pain and other changes in our bodies and in our life situations and relationships. Sometimes these changes are temporary; sometimes they are progressive.

Our physical and, we might add, our spiritual experiences are dynamic and forever changing. The frustration and discomfort that we feel emotionally and mentally could also be called dis-ease. If we are able to be fully present with our unique body's experiences, our unique life with all its challenges, then we could transform the dis-ease into ease. But how can we do that? We can turn to the mother of our physical experience, the spirit of our Mother Earth.

Imagine that you have developed diabetes. You are frustrated with the changes that your body and your life are presenting to you. You want to return to the past when you could eat candy as much as you wanted. You want to be able to go to a party and munch down what you used to eat. You want to feel more vitality. You want your old body's life. You want someone else's experience, someone else's body. You don't want to change your activities and habits. You don't want to take the medications and herbs. You don't want dietary changes. You are frustrated and envious of those who do not have this challenge, and of your old life without this challenge. You are in a disempowering state of dis-ease.

A helpful shamanic concept is that of 'Being With What Is' – being fully present in the moment. 'It is what it is,' say the Huichols of northern Mexico. To find help in 'being with what is' in your body and in your life, we suggest that you connect with the Spirit of Nature. She will help you to be in the physical flow of the Earth realm. We don't see the trees and the birds disempowered by their limitations, lamenting their 'lot in life'. Become One With – or in Harmony With – this spirit of Mother Earth.

One powerful way to do this is to connect with the elements, or with the spirit of a tree, or with the whole forest. Any spirit in nature will help you. It could be a spirit you know well or one that is new to you in journeytime. Experience being that spirit in journeytime. By experiencing life as that spirit and embodying that spirit's power in journeytime, you learn how you can call on that power in your everyday life.

JOURNEY: Your intention is to journey to a nature spirit and to merge with that spirit – with the spirit's permission of course.

Ask to find the spirit that will be the most help to you in your current situation, and if one does not appear, ask your guide(s) to take you to this spirit.

When you ISIS a spirit of nature before you, state why you have come and ask for permission to merge with the spirit. If you do not know what the spirit represents, ask. See yourself entering the spirit and becoming one with it. Be this spirit for a time, and notice how it feels, any messages that come and what happens in journeytime. Note who or what shows up. Of course, each journey is different and unique. Ask questions. Ask for assistance. You may call on your guide(s) if you wish. This journey is a powerful one where you can viscerally feel the qualities that the spirit possesses and find those qualities you wish to incorporate into your everyday life, or those you can call upon intermittently at times of need. To demonstrate, we will describe this merging journey with a physical illness or dis-ease, but we suggest that the 'Merging – Becoming One With' journey is something you can do many times within your shamanic practice and with as many spirits as you are called on to merge with. You can call this 'ease' to you with the assistance of spirits that dwell all around you on Earth. With time and practice, it is our hope that you will be able to do this in any moment and wherever you are, without a drum, in an instantaneous journey that brings in the power of nature to root your spirit in the Earth realm in a place of acceptance and grace, of 'ease', balance, wisdom and power.

We have all experienced dis-eases in our physical life. By our actions, many of them can be lessened or even eradicated. But what about those illnesses that cannot be cured or alleviated? Can the shamanic journey help heal those who have incurable dis-eases? We believe so. Sometimes by restoring body and spirit, sometimes by finding healing within the changed situation that the soul and spirit find themselves housed in.

Being dis-ease free is not always the same as eradicating a condition. Healing means Being One With What IS – with life and all its flowing changes, and even with the end of the physical as well, with what we call death. Being in harmony is being at ease rather than at DIS-ease. The easiest way to explain is by giving you an example. Christopher Reeve is an example of being healed without being cured:

In May of 1995, while participating in an equestrian event,

Christopher Reeve had an accident that resulted in paralysis for the remainder of his life. At the time of his spinal cord injury, most people would have said that for him to be healed he would have had to return to life as it was prior to the accident. He would have had to be able to get up and walk away from the wheel chair. Christopher could have spent the rest of his life being angry – angry at himself, at his 'present lot in life,' at the doctors, at his helpers, at his family and friends, at the world and at God. He could have spent the rest of his life lashing out at anyone or anything in order to vent the anger that comes after a sudden disability. He could have even ended his life or wished that he could die. All of this could also be said for his wife. But they didn't do these things. Instead, they made the important choice to live in the moment, each and every moment, fully present with what is, fully present with their unique experience in this life. They faced their moments each and every day with courage and determination. Severely limited, their lives completely changed from the way it WAS. They lived with the 'what IS' with grace, refusing to sink into dis-ease. Christopher Reeve founded The Christopher Reeve Foundation, co-founded The Reeve-Irvine Research Center, and lobbied on behalf of all people suffering from spinal cord injuries as well as for embryonic stem cell research. They accepted invitations for interviews, appeared at the Academy Awards in 1996, and hosted the Paralympics in Atlanta. Indeed, they reached out with such courage, grace and determination, doing so much for those living with similar life challenges, that his work was recognized by Time Magazine when in August, 1996, Christopher's picture was placed on the cover. Christopher and his wife went on to live the remainder of their lives with passion and compassion, accomplishing more on Earth than many of us without these severe physical challenges.

The reason we mention this is to give an inspiring example of finding ease in the face of severe dis-ease. And also to demonstrate that by ease, we do not mean easy. We mean living fully with what is and with the changes that come to us in our experience as physical beings. Living fully in the present, flowing as our life flows, and finding passion and purpose in life (and may we say in death as well), is being at ease with what is. In order for a person with any dis-ease to cope and move forward in their lives, they must live in the present. They must face the world from a 'What is' point of view. It appeared that Christopher found a great deal of strength and courage from his family and friends, and also from within himself. He was, in all aspects, a hero. Can the rest of us face our dis-eases with the same courage that he did? Perhaps not, but it behooves us to take note. Our lives will be all the more ecstatic and meaningful if we follow the example that the Reeves and so many others living under challenging conditions – whether physical, emotional or situational – have shown us. The following journey is a first step in beginning to accept the 'What is' philosophy regardless of the challenges you currently face, or those that will come to you in your life, relationships and situations.

JOURNEY: Your intention is to find the source of your dis-ease, and to find ease by becoming one with the flow.

Though sometimes difficult, this journey is powerfully transformative.

After stating your intention, ask your guide or spirit to take you to your dis-ease. Once you perceive it, ask the questions below that feel important. Ask what comes to you in your heart. Listen to the answers carefully and be attentive to everything that you ISIS in your journey. When you feel ready, ask the spirit of the dis-ease permission to merge with it and become one with it. Experience its energy and try to understand it. Notice if you find this a simple or difficult task. If difficult, ask for help from your guide(s) or spirit and ask what barriers are blocking this merging and what information or energy you need to help you to merge in order to experience Being the spirit of the challenge that you are exploring.

By now you have experienced some difficult journeys, and so you have many techniques that you can employ if needed. If afraid of the dis-ease and hesitant, do the Soul Hiding journey. Making Fear an Ally may be also helpful. If there is still fear, ask your guide to accompany you. If you still do not wish to, or are unable to enter the spirit of the dis-ease, then simply continue the conversation separately. This may be exactly where you need to be in order to gain the most from this journey. As in our everyday world, in journey world we have learned to trust that sometimes the most beneficial place to be is With What Is.

Remember, your notion of the severity of the dis-ease should not affect what you ask. Some of the questions that we suggest are:

Q: What is the source of my dis-ease?

Q: Why have you entered my life?

Q: What lessons do (or did) you wish me to learn?

Q: What, if anything, have I done in this life (or in past lives) that opened the door for you to come to me?

Q: What do you bring to me? What are your gifts?

Q: Why can't I perceive them as gifts?

Q: What are the challenges that you bring me? You may think you already know the challenges, but ask this anyway as you may be surprised by the answer (your challenge may seem all physical, but you may find that the answer is more relational or spiritual). As a generality, it is always good to ask questions you think you know the answer to in order to see what information is available for you from the perspective of other dimensions.

Q: Are there any actions I can take that will allow you to leave me now? While asking this last question, note how you feel. Try to get a sense as to whether it is time to move away from this way of being, or whether your soul has a need to live with this challenge for a time, or even permanently. It is important to note that if there is a strong emotional overlay, it may be difficult for you to get a true sense of this. If you hold a preconceived fear of this condition, you can ask spirit for help in asking the fear to open up the door to understanding so that you can stand in the condition fully, whether just for now in journeytime, or for the rest of your life. We suggest you not get bogged down with the notion of how long this condition will be with you. This can invoke fear in and of itself and block answers and power from coming through. Also, know that if you are listening with ears of fear or hope you may be blocked from truly hearing the answers. As you gain practice and the trust of your guides and the spirit world of journeytime, you will be able to sense the difference between your hopes and fears and spirit's answers. Even experienced journeyers, when faced with emotionally charged conditions, should take note and take their time asking questions, checking in with their heart, guides and higher self; utilizing whatever journey methods you have developed to access and communicate with spirit.

If you sense a 'Yes', that there are actions to take to get this condition to leave, ask what actions to take, both in journeytime and in everyday life, and what you must sacrifice, first in spirit reality and then in everyday reality.

If you sense a 'No,' ask:

Q: What must I know in order to live my life in the present – with you being a part of each moment in that present?

Q: What must I know about you in order to become one with you?

Q: How can I accept, and what must I do, to accept your nature and the fact that you are going to be a part of my future?

Q: How can I accept that future and maintain harmony with the world around me and with my higher self?

As with all journeys, these questions are just our suggestions. Please ask the ones that, deep in your heart, you know are to be asked and answered. Also, break these questions up in any order you deem most important to you and then do several journeys until you understand all that you need in order to move forward in your life. Repeat the journey again over time if you feel the need to as conditions change, and return to find the wisdom, power and energy that you need to live in this physical life with ease.

The Energy of Beauty

Beauty is a warm energy that radiates in and around a person that creates an appealing quality. Warmth, genuineness and connection make attraction for me. Nothing is more beautiful than a deep eye connection that speaks volumes while a verbal conversation is going on. Physical beauty is empty without the warmth...

Margulies

Physical attraction is a complex subject. In general, however, the more we embody spirit, the more present we are. The more we can bask in this presence, the more our energy shifts and we find we are BEING rather than BECOMING – able to give all those in our lives full and warm attention. We are truly present. This is beauty.

We all play with the adorning of our bodies to some extent, and much of this housekeeping is about comfort, health and hygiene. Whether we are bathing, applying balms or aromas, cutting our hair, shaving or cutting our nails, we are adorning our bodies. What we do with our bodies is an opportunity for playful embodiment of spirit. Whether applying makeup, wearing flowing clothes that appeal to us, matching (or purposely mismatching) colors and textures, and carefully placing jewelry and stones of differing colors and vibrations, we are enhancing our spirit's home – our body. In this way we deepen our connection with Mother Earth, connecting consciously from spirit to body to Earth. In everyday life, try being conscious of the energetic and spiritual effects when you are adorning your body and your surroundings. Note the effect on your senses and find conscious ways to enhance your senses with intent.

JOURNEYS: Your intention is to embody spirit and connect

deeper and deeper to Earth and Sky, bringing in true beauty.

These journeys span the bridge between journeytime and everyday life. Begin with journeytime in altered state, and then continue the journeys in conscious everyday time.

You can, of course, give these journeys as much time as you feel you need and want. Some may call to you more than others; pick and choose as you wish.

1. Stand or sit. Feel the earth firmly below you. Send your attention down to the core of earth, pulling up this Earth energy in to the area of your heart. Now, feel the sky above. Send attention up and out into the cosmos, pulling in the cosmic energy to your heart. Feel the intersection and melding of this power (Earth and Cosmos) in your heart. Next, send this powerful energy out from your heart and expand your attention of this outward energy. Expand more and more with each breath. Each time you do this you will strengthen your ability to fill from Source and your ability to radiate this source energy outwards.
2. Same as 1 only while feeling the earth and cosmic energies meld in your heart, feel this energy as sacred love in the form of a flower. Feel this flower as a bud which then expands and opens, more and more with each breath. Take in the combined energy of Earth, Sky and sacred love. Your physicality is the sacred union of the matter from Mother Earth and the light energy from Father Sun. Consciously Be the energy of that loving union.
3. Same as 1 only feel this sacred love energy rise to your eyes and expand outward, shining through your eyes more and more with each breath.
4. We all know that when someone is in love they radiate beauty. How many times has a friend come into the room and you know right away that they are in love just by the energy they are radiating. Or when you yourself were in

love and looked into a mirror to see a very different you looking back. Pure Beauty!

This journey is to Be in love. To Live in love. Begin by bringing to mind and heart and body a time when you were in love. It may be a time when you were in love with a special person in your life, or it can be a time when you felt love in your heart for any being or experience. It might be a time spent cuddling with your puppy, or that feeling of holding your baby for the first time – becoming lost in each other's eyes. Perhaps a time you got up early to see the sun rise over a lake, or paused in awe of the mists on the mountain as you climbed upwards. Bring in a time when you realized that you were brimming with energetic connection with the world, when your senses were heightened and brightened. This is love, not something that you wait to happen (waiting to find 'the one' – that special person to fall in love with – the one who can bring love out in you). Love is a choice that you can bring into your life and being. You can live in this expanded, heightened and connected state throughout your life. Feel this love energy wash all over you. Feel this become you. Walk with this energy. Feel it expand outward, more and more each time, both in journeytime and in walking through your everyday life. BE this energy and recall this feeling as often as you need to again and again. The more you do this journey, the more you can BE expansive love in every moment: one on one with the important people in your life, when meeting strangers, when in line at the grocery store, when driving on the highway – Living In Love.

5. Imagine a feeling of nourishment, of energetic satiety. Full physically, full in your heart, full in your mind, full in spirit. Be nourished, overflowing with this energy, and walk in life in that nourishment, calling it in whenever

needed.

6. Scan your skin. Feel it as silky smooth. Polish it, smoothing it more and more with each breath. Do this for your body in general. Feel any part, whether a surface part or a deep one, that is calling for energy, for molding, for healing, for filling. In journeytime, do whatever you sense needs to be done to repair whatever needs repairing. Reshape and reenergize each part. Play with it. Artfully remodel and rejuvenate the body that houses your spirit and soul.
7. Imagine yourself lying on a beach. As the waves come in, imagine them washing away all your stress, anger and all that you wish to release. Imagine all of this falling away more and more with each wave. If you like, as each wave pulls away, imagine a specific issue, energy or emotion that you wish to release leaving with the wave. Thank it as you ISIS it going. Thank these energies for the lessons that they have taught to you and say farewell, explaining that it is time that they leave so that you can experience life anew. Remember to ask that they rejoin the Universal Energy flow and trust Source to transmute the energy in a good way.

10. Bring your attention to your genitals. Feel the blood flowing and engorging powerfully, expanding and growing. Feel the juices flow, expanding like a pool beneath a waterfall. Take your attention to your heart. Feel the passion here as a sacred fire. Feed the embers of this fire, building more and more with each breath. Feel this sacred fire rise up through and out of your heart, then through and out of your eyes, down and expanding outward from your genitals, heart and eyes more and more with each breath. Feel the flow of energy from sacred genitals to sacred heart and feel this energy cycle round and round. Cycling and then expanding outward from the heart, expanding more and more each breath, cycling

> through this circuit and up to your eyes, cycling through genitals, heart and eyes. Feel the energy flow out of the eyes, radiating in all directions, forwards and behind and all around, expanding more and more with each breath. Again, the more you practice, the more you can walk in the world radiating this sacred fire and empowering others to rekindle their own fire. You know what they say about fire though – be careful or you might get burned. Keep your intent clear when you walk in the world with this energy, for it can be a very powerful attraction. Others may want to bask in this energy, and so it requires walking consciously with integrity and clear intent. The cleanest and most pure intent would be that of empowering others. Be careful of self-aggrandizement, and of course seduction is always to be undertaken with careful and clear mutual intent.

As you repeat these journeys, your energy shifts and inner beauty builds. This is the beauty of the Universe. Like moths to a flame, people are attracted to the radiance of inner beauty. We are attracted to those who are all out BEING rather then trying to be. It is a good practice to bring in source with any of these methods before you walk into a room. As you master this state of BEING BEAUTY, our hope is that you will notice a shift in how you relate to others, empowering and enlightening both yourself and the world around you, and Walking in Beauty.

Honing Your Inner Shaman – Using Nature's Healing Tools

Earlier in this text, we quoted our teachers, the wise elder Ipupiara Makunaiman and his powerful wife, Claicha Toscano. Ipupiara always tells his students, 'We are all shamans'. And he means it! He reminds us that each of us has within our hearts the same potential as shamans who have been doing this work all their lives. The journeys associated with this section are meant to connect with our shamanic core – to bring out the shamanic talent that each of us possesses.

We also mentioned that in each of our ancestral bloodlines, if you go back far enough, there are shamanic relatives (see Finding Your Inner Indigenous Self). This indigenous way of being is rooted in our nature and can be accessed by our intent.

It is not the purpose of this book to go into shamanic healing techniques used by our indigenous teachers; however, we would like to mention a healing technique here in order for you to fully understand the intent and purpose for this journey.

A mainstay in Ipupiara, Claicha and Eve's healing sessions is the use of fresh (raw and in their shell) eggs. By rubbing the eggs over their client's body, the egg acts as a sponge, absorbing energy and sucking out that which no longer serves the higher good of the client. Other items which they use besides the eggs are carnations or other flowers, branches, stones, candles, feathers and crystals to name a few. There are many shamanic tools that can be used, and the tools that shamanic communities the world over use depend on their local physical environment. Tools, of necessity, are different in a mountainous community from those in a rainforest or in a desert; however, they are always taken from nature. Their role is to provide a tangible connection between the shaman, his or her client, and the source of the tool's power – the Spirit of Mother Earth, known as Pachamama in

Claicha's Quechuan tongue. The word you use to name Source does not matter. The most important thing to remember is that the healing energy from the tool does not originate from the shaman him or herself, or from the tool. Neither shaman nor the tools they use are powerful. Any verbalized power from the shaman is, in our opinion, borne within the ego. The power lies totally within Great Spirit, within Source. Both shaman and tool are intermediaries, and how well the power is channeled depends on the relationship and connection that has been carefully and persistently built between shaman, tool and Source over time.

In modern times, we often just find or buy a healing object and begin to use it. A better way is to develop a deep relationship with the spirit of the tool first. The Zulu of South Africa, for an example, divine by throwing 'bones'. These are a group of objects, many of them actual bones, which are thrown to show the sangoma (the Zulu term for a healer or 'shaman') what is going on, and what to do about it. An apprentice sangoma will carry his or her first bone with them day and night for months and sometimes years before getting a second one. A relationship is developed with each bone which then shows them how it will be used and what it has to communicate. To gather a basket of a couple of dozen divining bones can take a very long time, to say the least.

JOURNEY: Your intention is to ask Spirit how you can use the natural objects that are found in your area. This journey can be done anywhere, even in an urban setting, for all of Mother Earth is sacred. You may be given information as to how to use natural objects in healing yourself or others. (You may even be given ways to help heal nonhuman entities, animals, the weather, Earth… Be open to the information you receive as always.)

Begin as you choose. Ask your guide(s) to show you what objects in your environment you could use for healing. As always, go with the flow and allow spirit or your guide to show you whatever they wish. The object(s) might be in your home, your backyard, in a park, whatever and wherever spirit directs you to.

After an item is identified, ask:

Q: Why have you shown me this item?
Q: How may I use this item in healing?
Q: How long am I free to use this tool? Once? Many times?
If this is a tool to be used multiple times, ask:
Q: How should I cleanse the item between each healing?
Q: How can I develop a relationship with this tool over time?
Q: How can I develop a flow between the tool, myself, Source and the client?
Q: How can I honor this tool?
Q: Where and in what manner may I keep this tool when it is not in use?
Q: When it is no longer to be used for this purpose, where would it like to be placed? Back to the Earth? In a fire? In a river? (Note that if no answer to this question comes now, you may journey to ask again when the time comes to let the tool go.)

The questions will, of course, depend on the tool, and on the previous answers.

If the answer is that it is to be used in divination or diagnosis, other questions will come to mind:

Q: Am I to collect a group of divination tools, or just the one?
Q: What is the symbology of the item? What is it telling me?
Q: Does the message depend on the position of the tool? (Depending on the item, is it to be thrown, held like a pendulum, etc?)
Q: Is the item to be used as both a diagnostic and therapeutic

tool? (i.e. for divination and for healing as well?)

In general, all tools should be taken from and returned to nature with gratitude. A gift of cornmeal or tobacco is always a wonderful way to thank Spirit for assisting in the healing process. However, the ways of giving thanks are not limited to these sacred plants. Be open to sensing other ways to give back in order to honor and show your gratitude to Source and to the tool.

You may have to repeat this journey in order to find out about all the items spirit may show you.

Many times, people collect gifts from nature long before they begin a shamanic path. If you have items in your home that you have picked up during your life's journey – stones, crystals, small pieces of driftwood, or any other gifts that you are already connected to – ask spirit to first show you how you can use these items in your healing. The fact that these items called to you, are in your home, and are bathed in your energies already makes them perfect tools for your shamanic practice. You already have a connection with them and this connection can be deepened and strengthened with use, honor and intent.

JOURNEY: Your intention is to communicate with the spirit of the plants or other natural objects in your environment to find out how they wish to be used in healing.

This is especially helpful for those who use herbs in healing and who gather their own herbs. Others, however, may also be shown locally available seasonal plants and foods for certain healing purposes. Once the use is obtained from the plant, it can be bought when needed by those who are not willing to directly harvest and prepare plant medicine. Even plants in your lawn or window pot may be called to give of themselves. The deeper the connection between the healer and the tool, as always, the more powerful the tool. Because of this, directly harvesting and preparing your medicinal healing plants is always best.

In indigenous communities, such as the rainforest, the number of plant choices available is mind-boggling. That certain usages and combinations would be found by trial and error is mathematically improbable. In fact, if you ask the healers in the area, they will tell you that they communicate with the spirit of the plants to find out how they wish to be used for any particular purpose or need within the community.

In our allopathic drug culture, even alternative healing modalities look for the 'silver bullet', going to great lengths to obtain plants from far away, harvesting these plants to the point of extinction, processing them beyond recognition, marketing them widely and transporting them across long distances. The more Earth-honoring, indigenous way would be to communicate with local seasonal plants to find out how they would like to be used.

Begin as you choose. (You can do this journey indoors in dreamtime, or by walking around your local gardens, hills, woods, park, garden or lawn, pausing in front of each tree or plant and journeying to them one on one, touching them to deepen the connection.) Ask to be taken to the plants in your area that are willing to be utilized in healing. Ask questions, and remember to give thanks:

Q: How would you like to be used?

Q: How would you like to be prepared – fresh or dried, as a tea, a salve, a bath, a poultice, a sachet?

Q: When would you like to be used and for what condition(s)?

Q: When and how would you like to be harvested (Season, lunar cycle, day or night...)?

Q: Which parts (bark, leaves, roots, whole plant, seeds, fruit etc.) may I use?

Q: Would you like to be combined with other plants? If yes, which plants?

Q: What can I give back in thanks?

Q: How can I support the remaining plant, or other plants present, and the environment?

An important note: UNLESS you are a trained herbalist or have knowledge outside of the shamanic journey in the uses and risks of herbs and plants, we suggest you DO NOT ingest any plant that is not a known food. If, in journeytime, you are given a use for a non-food plant that includes ingestion, we suggest you first consult an herbalist.

Spirit's Perspective on My Issue

The main intent of this journey is for you to examine the true nature of a problem that you are seeking information about. This is particularly helpful when you feel 'stuck' in order to see if your mind is amplifying the problem. Major insights can be gleaned very quickly through this journey when you come across, and dialog with, the image of your problem that you imagine, see, intuit or sense.

JOURNEY: Your intention is to ask Spirit how she/he views (your problem).

Begin as you choose. Then, ask your guide or call out to spirit from your safe place: 'Show me a representation of (my problem) not as I see it, but as you see it.'

When you begin to sense what shape the problem is talking in journeytime, you will understand the problem's true form from spirit's perspective, and the message that spirit is giving you. It is our belief that the shape it will take will allow you to ISIS exactly how spirit views the issue. Using 'shyness' as the example problem; imagine that you feel that your shyness is so overpowering that it governs your every move. But when called upon in journeytime with the above intention, a mouse, not a giant, appears. What does that say to you? What insights and information do you sense even before you begin to dialog with the spirit of the 'shyness' mouse? It would be arrogant of us to try to tell you what spirit's message is for you at any given moment, but in this example it may mean that you have not been in touch with the messages spirit has been trying to give you. Take note when something completely unexpected is experienced in journeytime - those may be very important messages. We suggest you don't rush through those unexpected moments, but spend as much time as you need to understand what it is that you have ISISed.

Ask questions and call in your guide(s) for help when it feels appropriate.

To continue with this hypothetical example, Spirit may know that the shyness is holding you back, not because it really is a major spiritual issue for you, but because you have chosen to make it one. No matter how restrictive it feels to you in everyday reality, this shyness is not as huge in spirit world as your mind will have you think it is. Your soul and spirit may have other 'ways of being' in our everyday world and those ways may be available to you already. Your true authentic self may not be shy at all. It may be that spirit is giving you the message to let this issue go, that it is not important. This information can reinforce your resolve to make new choices and put the shyness in its proper place.

Conversely, in this example, if a giant appears, then spirit may be confirming to you that this is a huge challenge for you in this life, or that you have allowed shyness to grow in all aspects in all realities. If this is the case, you can employ any number of journeys already discussed in this text in order to begin to transform the shyness.

But, we just said that it would be arrogant of us to try to tell you what spirit's message is for you at any given moment. What if what we just said above is not the message? Earlier in the text, we spoke about how dis-ease may manifest itself in spirit reality before any symptoms appear in everyday reality. The giant shyness may be the precursor of what your shyness will become if you do not begin to change the shape and energy of the shyness in both realities. How can you discover the real nature of the message that the image is trying to portray to you in your journey? Question it. Ask your guides if you cannot understand the information. Merge with it and feel the energy. See the issue from its own perspective.

Remember, spirit world and physical Earth are one. By shifting to a harmonious state in journeytime, you open the door for healing to occur in everyday reality. ISISing spirit's scope of the issue will help you to decide the importance of taking time and energy with this problem, and will help you find what, if anything, must be shifted and what actions taken, both in journeytime and/or in everyday reality.

Much information can be garnered from this journey; however, once you sense the shape of the issue, you may already have the information you need. If you feel unsure, ask questions. Possible questions, regardless of the problem:

Q: Why do I view you so differently from the way you have come to me today?

Q: What steps must I take in everyday reality to live aligned with and in harmony with you?

Q: How can I better hear the message(s) spirit has for me when I am in everyday life?

Q: What must I do to support you the way you are, not the way I perceive you?

The rest of the questions, if any, are up to you in the moment.

If you encountered a big discrepancy between what you expected and what appeared in the previous journey, you might try the next one.

JOURNEY: Your intention is to shift your problem to align your everyday life with your spiritual life.

Begin as you choose (or alternatively, simply continue within the above journey). Ask the spirit form of your problem as it has appeared to you, or your guide(s), what is keeping you from living in full alignment with your guides or higher Self - what is causing the discrepancy between the way you perceive the problem and the way it has come to you in journeytime. Depending on what you ISIS in the moment, take action in journeytime to change this. For an example, if a wall appears, you may break it to smithereens with a mallet. If gooey, slimy poison flows from or near you, you may ISIS the toxins transmuting into juicy, nutritious mangos. You get the picture. Ask also what you can do in everyday life to align more closely with Spirit and to hear the messages as they are given.

If you feel that your mind is creating 'mountains out of molehills' so to speak, you may want to try the next journey to align your heart and mind. We, in the industrialized nations, are very developed in our upper chakras, with incredibly powerful intellect. This is wonderful, unless it creates problems through imbalanced mind-chatter and worry.

One of Eve's teachers, the Quichuan Yachag Alberto Taxo, would always tell Americans who came to him, 'Feel – Don't Think'. This was a very helpful mantra to begin to try to live more from the heart rather than the head. Imagine Eve's surprise when she went with him as he spoke to a group of Quichuans one day and he said to them, 'Think – Don't Feel'. Their imbalance was in living through their emotions without thinking about the consequences. A good mantra for balance is 'Feel your feelings, think your thoughts, don't think about your feelings or feel your thoughts.'

JOURNEY: Your intention is to find balance by aligning heart and mind.

Begin as you choose. Ask your guide(s) or spirit what is keeping you from aligning heart and mind. ISIS your heart, your mind and the connection or block. Again, depending on what you ISIS, you may be able to begin to breakdown the block in journeytime and build the connection. Ask what can be done in everyday life to build and maintain the connection, to strengthen your heart if your mind is stronger, and to find balance; to listen to your heart, and open your mind to its voice.

Minor Life Events That Aren't Minor

We can all identify events in our lives that triggered major shifts in us. Some of these were very happy ones – some traumatic. But what about the in between times? We don't live day-to-day waiting for major life events. We get up every morning and do whatever we have to do – go to school, to our job, or to tackle all the chores that await us. And we don't live in a vacuum. Each day, we interact with other people and other people interact with us. And each and every one of those interactions affects us, in some cases altering our very being and how we behave, both in the moment and in the future. These interactions have energy and through them we weave the energetic web of who we are as individuals, and we weave the web that is our community. When woven consciously, this forms a beautiful energetic fabric. Yet most of us are not fully present and conscious of the importance of our energetic flow in each moment.

It is exactly because we were not fully conscious of our energetic flow in past moments that events which changed us may not have seemed earth shaking at the time – and that these shifts in our being may have progressed unnoticed, resulting in dis-ease. Our hope is that the following journeys will help to identify and change these shifts, and will help to engender conscious energetic presence.

JOURNEY: Your intention is to ask spirit to show you an event or interaction in your life that had a major effect on you, even though you did not realize the pivotal nature of the event at that moment.

Begin as you choose. When you have connected with your spirit guide or are securely within your safe place, make your intention known. Now, just like the journey to your shadow self, experience the event or interaction that comes up in journeytime.

Just 'be' with the event; ISIS it. Your goal during this part of the journey is to find out why spirit deems this a major event for you. Many times, this realization instantly reveals itself to you in some way, and in this case the answers to the questions posed below will be blatantly obvious. If not, when it feels appropriate, we suggest you ask the following questions of your guide, to spirit in general, or to what/who ever you ISIS in the journey:

Q: Why was this event pivotal?
Q: How has the event altered my life?
Q: What would my life have looked like if this event had never happened?
Q: What might I have learned from this event had I been fully conscious of the significance to me and of the shifts occurring?
Q: Specifically, what dis-ease, if any, manifested in me that began or progressed with this event?
Q: What can I do to learn the lesson the event was to teach me?
Q: What can I do in everyday reality to change the dis-ease that the event has manifested, and return to harmony with my higher Self and with the Universe?

JOURNEY: Your intention is to ask for assistance in being fully present in every moment to the nature of the energetic shifts occurring.

Begin as you choose. Ask your guide(s) to come for assistance, or ask spirit in general if this is your preference. Ask for help in being present in everyday reality, and what you can do to be conscious of the energetic shifts occurring moment by moment, with each event and interaction. Ask for a specific cue from spirit to remind you to focus on the present and on the energetic shifts occurring at times when it may be important. Alternatively, you could give spirit a cue that feels like it would be easy for you to notice, perhaps an itch in your left ear, or something red to appear, or whatever you choose as your signal. This journey may be repeated over time to continue to ask for deeper levels of assistance as you become more and more conscious of the web, of your point in the web, and of your effect on the web.

Spiritually Walking Through Physical Life by Embodying Spirit

By now you will have heard us say many times that, although we are spiritual beings having a physical experience, there is no true separation between the spiritual and physical. What affects one affects the other. And yet we often live in a state of artificial disconnection. The more we can truly embody our spirit, the more we can walk in this physical world we call life fully conscious of the experience, wisdom, power and energy of spirit - the more vitality and life purpose we can realize.

There are many previously described journeys that can help you to come to this state of spiritually walking through physical life – of embodying spirit. In fact, virtually all journeys help with this.

If you have not done these journeys before, you might try them now:

Shifting Dis-ease to Ease – to come to terms with your body and the way it is changing over time.

Journey to Past Lives – to imagine what gifts this body brings to you, what purpose you might have for this particular body and what it might have been like in another body.

Journey to Your Essence, the Junction of Soul and Spirit – to connect with those who walked before you in your bloodline, who passed your body to you, and those to whom you are spiritually and physically connected through the ages.

Finding Your Inner Indigenous Self (Restoring Connection and Harmony While Living with Gratitude and Honor) – to find and deepen your connection with the physical realm.

In this section we will describe a few more journeys that can help us to consciously allow our soul and spirit to inhabit our bodies, and this sensory physical Earth plane.

We have talked a great deal in this book about the shamanic

Earth honoring way of life. Remember to give gratitude and honor to your piece of the Earth that houses your soul and spirit – your body.

JOURNEY: Your intention is to journey to your body, giving thanks, sending love and energy to each part.

Begin as you choose. ISIS yourself traveling through your body, from top down or bottom upwards, spending time with each part. Feel how it has been for your skin, eyes, nose, bones, heart, lungs, arms, feet... to go through each day and night, from birth to death, housing your spirit and soul and following the commands from your brain, expressing your desires and dreams through your nervous system. Give thanks to each area; send loving energy and listen to any messages. You may find that certain body parts have something to ask of you, and may require a commitment from you in order to maintain optimal functioning. Give thanks to your ancestors and to the Earth and Sky. As always, repeat this journey as needed to take good care of your body-house.

JOURNEY: Your intention is to dialog with an area or organ of your body that is causing you difficulty in your life.

Begin as you choose. Ask your guide(s) or spirit to take you to the spirit of (name the body part). Alternatively, you could ask the spirit of the body part to take a form in journeytime and dialog directly with it. Listen to what the part has to say. Hear the messages that it holds. Ask questions. We suggest:

Q: What are you feeling?
Q: What message(s) do you hold for me?
Q: What information?
Q: How does your situation affect other body parts?
Q: My life as a whole?
Q: Are there choices that I made in the past that have harmed

you?

Q: What can I do to bring you into balance and optimal function, in journeytime?

Q: In everyday life?

You may also ask your guide(s) or spirit to take you to the part that you need to be with now (especially if you are not sure which part to speak to for the difficulty you are experiencing).

Be open to messages, as they may not always be what you are expecting. If you make a commitment to take action in everyday life, keep that commitment, and if you find it hard to make these changes, journey to your guide(s) and your body, heart, mind, spirit and soul for help. And, as always, if no message comes, try rephrasing the question and consider that you may not be ready for the answer. Ask if you should journey back later for an answer.

JOURNEY: Your intention is to journey to and experience your time of death in this life.

Those who have gone through near-death experiences almost unanimously describe a new relationship with death. Eve has heard many people tell their stories of dying and coming back, describing a real release of the fear of death. They describe a new relationship with death and even a sweet anticipation of the afterlife. This new relationship with death allows a freeing up of the energy previously used in fearfulness, and is described as feeling lighter, and of a heightened appreciation of the precious time on this planet. Near-death survivors say that they can live full out, in a way that they could never do before this experience with death. Many also describe receiving an understanding of the power that they hold, and of their purpose in this life.

We have described journeys to the future several times in this text. This progression (as opposed to regression) is particularly powerful as it allows you to have a good relationship with your death, without needing to have a severe injury. It may, however, be difficult for some. It is especially difficult for those who have suffered extreme grief, who associate the most painful emotion around death. It may well be, however, that these are exactly the people who will benefit the most from building a new relationship with death.

Your intention is not to find out when, where or how you will die, but rather to feel the feelings of ending your time on this Earth plane and leaving your body, and to build a relationship with the spirit of death.

Begin as you choose. Ask your guide(s) or spirit to take you to the time of your death in this life. Take time experiencing the energy and feeling the emotions that arise. You may ask the spirit of death to take a form, or simply ask questions if you feel the need to. The spirit of death may take any form, as is true of all spirits. Feel your soul and spirit leave your body. Pay attention to all around you, to the dark and light, to the spirits and souls, to those left behind on Earth.

At any time you may ask your guide(s) to bring you out of the experience if you feel you are not ready to handle it; however, it is our experience that we are able to handle more than we think we can if we stick to thinking our thoughts and feeling our feelings, rather than ruminating about our feelings and feeling our thoughts. It is also our experience that spirit will only take us when and where we are ready. It is good though, as always, to know that we do have a choice to go or to stay.

Eve says, 'It has been my experience that the portals of birth and death hold great power and are the most sacred of times. The spirit of death is a compassionate spirit that has always been graciously willing to converse and answer questions, bringing perspective, wisdom, power and energy to anyone asking for help in journeytime.'

JOURNEY: Your intention is to fully embody your soul and spirit here on Earth.

The Quichuan Andean Shaman, Don Alberto Taxo, has said that our five senses are the portal to spirit. If we have lived disconnected to the spiritual nature of our bodies, this may seem counterintuitive. And yet diving into the sensuality of life with spiritual intent heightens our consciousness and roots our soul and spirit in our bodies and in our lives.

Begin as you choose. Call in the guide(s) that are willing to help you embody spirit, and also those who are willing to be called upon when needed in everyday life. These will be your embodiment guide or guides. In journeytime, ISIS each sense. Spend as much time with each sense as you feel is needed.

Smell - freshly mown grass, the forest, the ocean, peaches, tangerines, dirt, roses... Note the spirit of the smells that came to you today. Experience them deeply in spirit or journeytime. You can dialog with the spirit of smell if it feels right to you, or ask your guide(s) if you have questions.

When you have finished, move on to the next sense. Any order that comes to you is the order that you need. Alternatively, if you are directed to, you can do this in a single journey spending time with each sense, one after the other.

Hear - pealing bells, a harpsichord, raindrops on the roof, hoof beats, drums, music, fire crackling...

Taste - lemons, salt, beer, bitter greens, chocolate, hair, ice, creamed spinach, skin...

Touch - silk, sandpaper, sand spilling though your fingers, cold water, ice, warm water, gooey gel, hair, skin...

See - rainbows, mountains, oceans, grasslands, deserts, stars, glaciers, geometric shapes, colors...

There may well be messages in what you experience. There certainly will be power and energy. Ask. But most of all, experience what you ISIS. Become one with the energy. How can you keep that energy with you in your waking life? Ask your guide(s), or ask what you ISIS; ask the sense; ask the energy itself.

JOURNEY: Your intention is to experience spirit through body.

This journey is similar to the one above, and can be broken up into several journeys if it feels right. While deeply experiencing each sense with your physical body, bring spirit in. Ask permission of spirit and, if given, merge with and become one with whatever spirit comes to you. Ask for assistance from your embodiment guide. Some will find it best to give each sensation a day, a week or a month – whatever period of time feels right to you is good. In your everyday life, keep coming back to the presence of the sense that you journeyed to and bring that spirit in. What comes to your mind? Your heart? What emotions? What messages? What power? What energy? Feel your unique spiritual nature through each sense, and feel the way your spirit and soul are housed in the physical body. Be present to your spirit and to the realm of Spirit. As you walk in everyday life between worlds, fully presence your soul's experiences of these senses, and to the spirit of these senses, and ask yourself:

Are you more alive? Are you more aware? Are you walking in spirit? Are you spiritually embodied?

Epilogue

This is by no means a comprehensive list of journeys. In fact, a comprehensive list can never be made, as the possibilities for using the shamanic journey is limitless. It is our hope that having read this book, and experienced these journeys, your life has changed. Even more importantly, it is our hope that you now have the tools, and the deep connection with Earth and Spirit, that you need to enable you to forever walk a path that is in your higher good, and the higher good of all our relations. That you will walk communing with all on this Earth plane of 'everyday' life knowing that everything has spirit. That as you walk in spirit you will empower all those around you to also walk in spirit, connected, with honor and gratitude to Mother Earth and Father Sky and connected to Source. That you will remain open to communication, direction and assistance from Spirit, and that all our relations, Mother Earth and Father Sky benefit.